SYSTEMS DIRECT AUDITING PRACTICE CASE

Includes Lotus® 1-2-3® tutorial and template diskette

Dieter H. Weiss, PhD, CPA
Ferris State College
Big Rapids, Michigan

Gaylord N. Smith, CPA
Associate Professor
Albion College
Albion, Michigan

COLLEGE DIVISION South-Western Publishing Co.

CINCINNATI   DALLAS   LIVERMORE

Copyright © 1991
by South-Western Publishing Co.
Cincinnati, Ohio

ALL RIGHT RESERVED

The text of this publication, or any part thereof, may not be reproduced in any form or by any means, electronic or mechanical, including photocopying, recording, storage in an information retrieval system, or otherwise, without the prior written permission of the publisher.

ISBN: 0-538-80902-7

Library of Congress Catalog Number:n 90-60316

2 3 4 5 6 7 8 DH 7 6 5 4 3 2 1

Printed in the United States of America

Lotus and 1-2-3 are registered trademarks of Lotus Development Corporation.

Cover illustration by Lonni Sue Johnson

CONTENTS

Disk file name is shown within parenthesis

INTRODUCTION
Overview of Practice Set Assignments	2
Background	3
Permanent File	3
Organization Chart	4
Floor Plan, Detroit Location	5
List of Employees	6
Chart of Accounts	7
Minutes of Meetings of Board of Directors/Stockholders	8
Lease Agreement	11
Report of Certified Public Accountants	12
Prior Years' Balance Sheets (Prybs. wk1)	13
Prior Years' Income Statements (Pryis. wk1)	14
Statements of Retained Earnings (Pryis. wk1)	15
Statement of Cash Flows (Cashflow.wk1)	15
Notes to Financial Statements	16
Engagement Letter	17
Working Trial Balance (Trialbal.wkl)	18
Recurring Monthly General Journal Entries (RGJ90.wk1)	20

ASSIGNMENT 1— GENERAL MATTERS
Audit Program	21
Time Budget Worksheet (Timebud.wk1)	22
Narrative of Operating Procedures	23

ASSIGNMENT 2— PETTY CASH AND REGULAR CASH ACCOUNT
Audit Program	27
Cash Lead Schedule (Cashlead.wk1)	28
Petty Cash (Pettycas.wk1)	29
Bank Reconciliation—Regular Account (Bankrec.wk1)	30
Bank Reconciliation—Payroll Account (Bankrecp.wk1)	31
Bank Confirmation Inquiry	32
Interbank Cash Transfers (Intbank.wk1)	33
Payroll (Payroll.wk1)	34
Selected Cash Receipts	35
Check Register—Selected Sections	36
Cutoff Bank Statements—Regular and Payroll Accounts	38
Bank Cutoff Analysis—Regular and Payroll Accounts (Cutanly.wk1)	39
Bank Deposit Tickets and Cancelled Checks	40

ASSIGNMENT 3—REVENUES AND RECEIVABLES
Audit Program	46
Schedule of Selling Prices of Equipment & Software	48
Receivables—Lead Schedule (Reclead.wk1)	49
Partial Sales Journal (Salesjou.wk1)	50
Sales Invoices—Selected	51

iii

Accounts Receivable:
    Equipment Subsidiary Ledger (Eqsubled.wk1)   61
    Comments on Equipment Confirmations   64
    Parts and Supplies   65
    Letters of Confirmation   66
Notes Receivable:
    Schedule of Notes Receivable (Notesrec.wk1)   78
    Notes Receivable Worksheet (Notrecws.wk1)   79
    Unrealized Gross Profit on Notes Receivable (Unrealgp.wk1)   80
Allowance for Doubtful Accounts:
    Notes from Management Inquires   81
    Allowance for Doubtful Accounts Worksheet (Allow.wk1)   82
    Calculation of Experience Ration (Allow.wk1)   83

ASSIGNMENT 4—INVENTORY, PAYABLE SAND COST OF SALES
Audit Program   84
Inventory—Lead Schedule (Invlead.wk1)   86
Equipment and Software
    Summary of Count Sheets (Inveneqp.wk1)   87
    Audit Memo   88
Parts and Supplies:
    Summary of Count Sheets (Invenp&s.wk1)   89
    Audit Memo   90
Interoffice Memo —Client's inventory instructions   91
Freight-In Allocation Worksheet (Freight.wk1)   93
Accounts Payable —Trade (Acctpay.wk1)   94
Purchase —Vendors, Invoices   95

ASSIGNMENT 5—OTHER CURRENT ASSETS (PREPAID EXPENSES)
Audit Program   104
Prepaid Expenses—Lead Schedule (Preplead.wk1)   105
Prepaid Expenses—Analysis (Prepexp.wk1)   106
Prepaid Insurance Schedule (Insuranc.wk1)   108
Letter from Acme Insurance Agency   109

ASSIGNMENT 6—PLANT, PROPERTY, AND EQUIPMENT
Audit Program   110
Plant, Property, and Equipment—Lead Schedule (Ppelead.wk1)   111
Depreciation Schedule (Deprsch.wk1)   113
Repairs and Maintenance—Analysis (Repairs.wk1)   114
Analysis of Fixed Asset Acquisitions and Depositions (Fixasset.wk1)   115
Vendors' Invoices   116
Lease Calculations (Leaseanl.wk1)   118

ASSIGNMENT 7—OTHER CURRENT LIABILITIES
Audit Program   119
Other Current Liabilities—Lead Schedule (Curllead.wk1)   121
Accounts Payable—Other (Acpayoth.wk1)   122
Accrued Expenses (Accruexp.wk1)   122
Salaries Expense, Employee Benefits

Payroll Tax Expense (Salpenpr.wk1)   123
Payroll Taxes Withheld and Accrued   125
Pension Obligation and Expense   125
Bonus and Income Tax Computations—from 1989 Workpapers (Bontax89.wk1) 126
Bonus and Income Tax Calculations—1990 (Bonustax.wk1)   127
Income Taxes Payable (Inctxpay.wk1)   129
Dividends Payable (Dividend.wk1)   130

ASSIGNMENT 8—LONG-TERM LIABILITIES
Audit Program   131
Long-Term Liabilities—Lead Schedule (Ltllead.wk1)   132
Mortgage Payable (Mortpay.wk1)   133
Lease Obligation (Leaseanl.wk1)   134
Interest Payable and Interest Expense (Interest.wk1)   135

ASSIGNMENT 9—STOCKHOLDERS' EQUITY
Audit Program   136
Stockholders, Equity—Lead Schedule (Skeqlead.wk1)   137
Stockholders (Stkhold.wk1)   138
Miscellaneous and Other Expense Accounts (Miscell.wk1)   139

ASSIGNMENT 10—COMPLETING THE AUDIT
Audit Program   140
AJE File (AJE.wk1)   141
Management Representation Letter   142
Attorney's Letter   144
Selected Ratios—Worksheet (Ratio.wk1)   145
Recurring General Journal Entries—1991 (RGJ91.wk1)   147

LOTUS 1-2-3 TUTORIAL   149
Index to Tutorial   181

INTRODUCTION

Systems Direct is an audit case designed to involve the student in an audit engagement like what he/she would experience in actual practice. This practice set embodies years of audit experience of the authors and is intended to simulate reality as closely as possible.

In addition to following audit procedures, you will learn sound workpaper techniques, practice writing letters, review notes to financial statements, and maintain a time budget for each phase of the audit. The case is intended for a one-semester or two-quarter course in auditing and requires 30 to 40 hours to complete.

You will assume the role of staff accountant with the Smith and Weiss CPA firm and given the responsibility of carrying out audit procedures and assignments as indicated by the audit programs. Some procedures have already been performed by an associate to reduce the time needed to complete the set. These are indicated by the initials DHW on the audit program and workpapers. In some workpapers, DHW has made audit notes and given guidance for completing those workpapers.

As you proceed through the audit, you may assume that adjusting journal entries will be accepted by the client only if the explanations are complete. The explanations should include supporting computations or refer to copies of workpapers which support the adjusting entries.

Adjusting entries should be written out in detail in the workpapers to which the entries pertain and in the Adjusting Journal Entries (AJE) file, where all adjusting entries are listed in numerical order. It is firm policy that all adjusting entries be rounded to the nearest dollar. Reference is made to the AJE in the lead schedule, workpapers, and trial balance work sheet.

In many audits, some degree of preliminary work is performed by the client, including preparation of various schedules and analyses as requested by the independent auditor. Such schedules are marked "PBC" (prepared by client). Upon receipt of such schedules from the client, the auditor will verify the mathematical accuracy of the calculations and will trace certain amounts to the underlying general and/or subsidiary ledger accounts. The performance of such procedures will be noted by appropriate tickmarks.

Tickmarks are a series of symbols that represent audit procedures performed. As you perform various procedures, you will leave your "footprints" by using tickmarks, thus enabling your instructor to review your performance on each aspect of the audit. To facilitate efficiency in workpaper review, your firm has adopted the following tickmark legend.

C	= confirmed (confirmation received).
CF	= crossfooted (added) the row.
E	= examined underlying document (invoice, statement, etc.).
F	= footed (added) column of figures.
T/B	= schedule balance agrees with the general ledger account balance as shown in the trial balance.
T	= traced posting from (or to) journal to (or from) ledger account.
V	= calculation verified.
( )	= use numbers or small letters to describe procedures not indicated above [i.e., (a), (b), (1), (2)]. Explain the meaning of the tickmark in a footnote at the bottom of the workpaper.

Included in this practice case is a form of time budget used in public accounting as a basis for charging staff time to clients. You should keep a record of time spent on each phase of the audit (to the nearest 1/4 hour) and submit these time budgets with each assignment so the instructor may record accumulated time spent on the audit.

At the completion of each assignment you are to turn in the items indicated after the audit program for each assignment.

OVERVIEW OF PRACTICE CASE ASSIGNMENTS

1. Review permanent file contents.
   Prepare flow charts from narrative descriptions, noting weaknesses in internal control to be included in the management letter.

2. Cash
   Prepare petty cash workpaper.
   Reconcile regular checking account.
   Reconcile payroll checking account.
   Bank cutoff statement included.

3. Receivables, Allowance, and Revenue Accounts
   Test sales cutoff.
   Test for errors in billing, prices, wrong accounts, extensions, etc.
   Handle confirmation exceptions.
   Review January collections.
   Compute balance in allowance account based on moving average experience ratio.
   Compute unrealized gross profit on installment notes for income tax calculation.

4. Inventory, Payables, and Cost of Goods Sold
   Test purchase cutoff.
   Allocate freight-in between inventory and cost of goods sold.
   Test for purchase discounts.
   Perform pricing tests.
   Test for obsolete inventory.
   Review January payment for unrecorded payables.

5. Other Current Assets: Prepaid Expenses [i.e., insurance, taxes, and professional services]
   Make adjusting entries to the prepaid and related expense accounts from the client's monthly journal entries.

6. Plant, Property, and Equipment [i.e., asset changes, depreciation, lease, gains/losses, and repairs and maintenance]
   Make adjusting entries to correct posting to repairs account, to correct recording of disposal and gain recognition, and to adjust the depreciation allowance and expense accounts.

7. Other Current Liabilities: Accrued Salaries, Bonuses, Taxes, Interest
   Make adjusting entries needed for accrued bonuses, taxes, and interest.
   Reclassify certain long-term liabilities as current.
   Review January check register for unrecorded liabilities.

8. Long-term Liabilities: Mortgage, Equipment Notes, Lease Obligation, Interest Expense
   Make adjusting entry needed to separate interest from principal in monthly payments, all of which were charged to the liability account.
   Reclassify into current portion of debt.
   Record long-term lease obligation and two monthly payments, and reclassify portion to current.

9. Stockholders' Equity
   Analyze selected expense accounts (example Miscellaneous Expense).
   Make final analytical review.

10. Completing the Audit
    Complete the work papers:
    1. Post adjusting entries to work sheet.
    2. Extend, foot, and crossfoot work sheet.
    3. Compute bonuses and income taxes.
    4. Prepare adjusting entries for bonuses and income taxes and complete work sheet.
    5. Note reclassification accounts (accounts to be combined for financial statement presentation).
    6. Index workpapers and reference accounts to workpapers.
    Representation letters:
    1. From management—student must draft appropriate letter given the AICPA Audit Standards.
    2. From attorney.
    Make subsequent events check.
    Prepare statements and report. (Note new Statement of Cash Flows format.)
    Draft management letter, including internal control weaknesses.

BACKGROUND

Systems Direct has been in business since 1982 at the same location outside Detroit, Michigan. During this period, the company has grown from a small local operation to a large regional firm serving retail outlets in four states. Initially, the company handled only stereos and various components of electronic sound equipment. However, with the development of the personal home computer, a new, expanded market emerged. Since personal computers complemented the existing product lines, it seemed natural for Systems Direct to add computers to their lines.

The founding stockholders of Systems Direct also serve as officers and are active in the operation of the business; therefore, the minutes are from meetings of both the officers and stockholders. Meetings are generally held quarterly.

As the business grew, additional personnel were hired as needed. There is very little turnover since the employees are well-treated. In fact, the officers are contemplating a profit-sharing plan in which all employees would participate.

Despite growth, the company has been slow to increase the number of accounting personnel or to modernize the record keeping and recording functions. The management letter prepared by the previous auditors called attention to the need to strengthen internal controls.

Your firm was appointed as auditors for 1990 at the October, 1989, meeting of the board of directors, succeeding Dewitt and Tanner, the auditors since Systems Direct began in business.

Representatives of your firm were present at the inventory taken during the last week of 1989 and made the usual test counts to avoid having to qualify the 1990 audit report.

The firm of Dewitt and Tanner has provided you with the permanent file and certain workpapers from 1989, which are included here.

The permanent file includes narrative descriptions of existing duties, functions, and controls of principal employees. The descriptions were obtained early in the year as part of the preliminary review. Because of expected continued growth of Systems Direct, your firm believes it is important to rely more heavily on internal controls in the future.

Accordingly, one of your first assignments is to prepare flowcharts of each of the functions described in the narratives, identify weaknesses in internal controls, and recommend measures to strengthen internal controls.

PERMANENT FILE

The permanent file includes the following:
- Articles of incorporation and by-laws (not shown here)
- Organizational chart
- Floor plan of Detroit location
- List of employees
- Chart of accounts
- Minutes from meetings of board of directors and stockholders
- Lease agreement
- 1989 financial statements and auditor's report.
- 1989 management letter, calling attention to weaknesses in internal control (not shown here).
- Engagement letter with Smith and Weiss, CPAs.
- Letter to Dewitt and Tanner, CPAs, authorizing them to provide Smith and Weiss with material from their files (not shown here).
- Tax file, including the various federal, state, and local tax returns and related material and correspondence (not shown here; is located in tax department of our firm).

SYSTEMS DIRECT ORGANIZATIONAL CHART
(1990 Salaries)

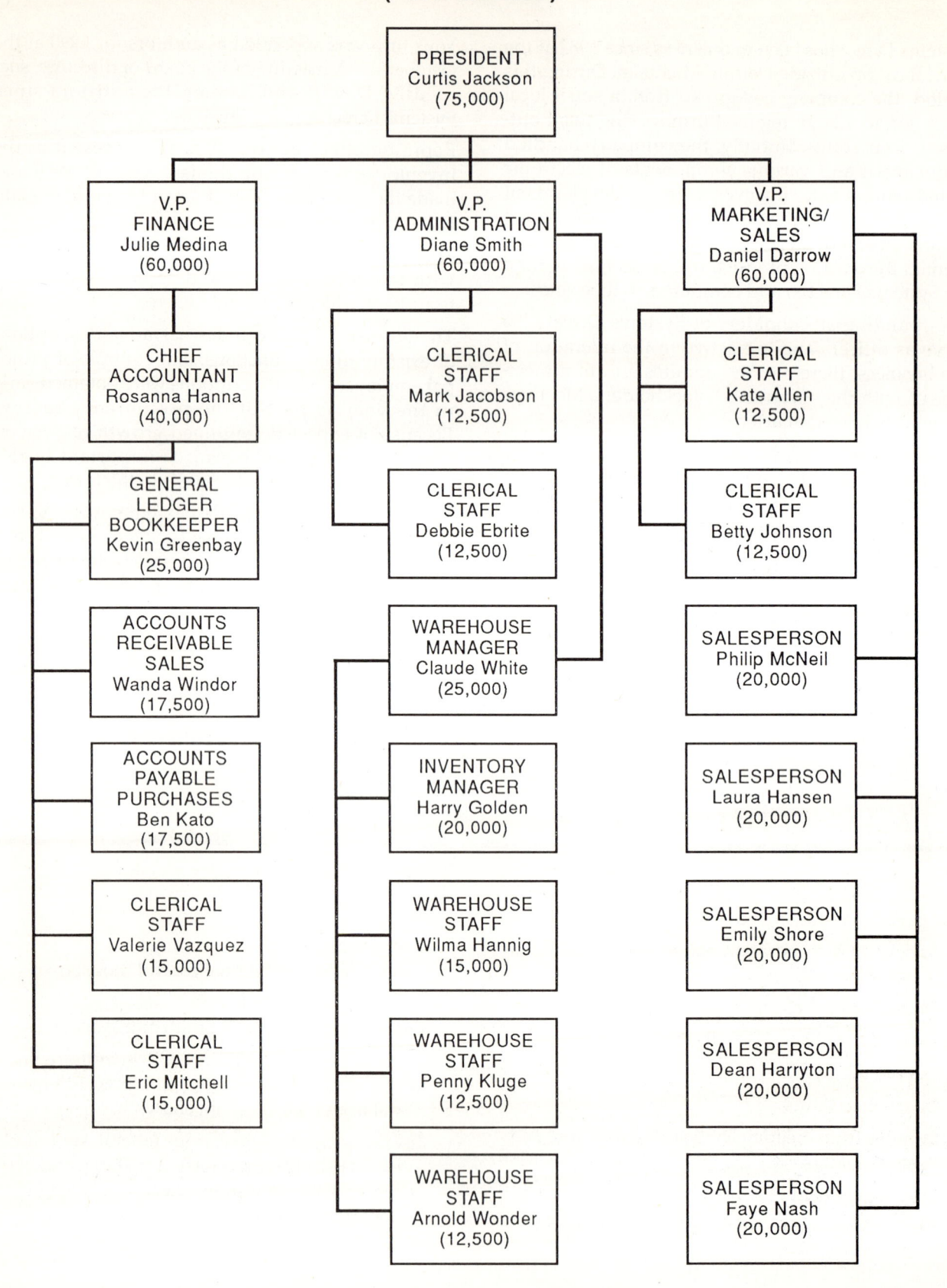

PRESIDENT
Curtis Jackson
(75,000)

V.P. FINANCE — Julie Medina (60,000)
- CHIEF ACCOUNTANT — Rosanna Hanna (40,000)
  - GENERAL LEDGER BOOKKEEPER — Kevin Greenbay (25,000)
  - ACCOUNTS RECEIVABLE SALES — Wanda Windor (17,500)
  - ACCOUNTS PAYABLE PURCHASES — Ben Kato (17,500)
  - CLERICAL STAFF — Valerie Vazquez (15,000)
  - CLERICAL STAFF — Eric Mitchell (15,000)

V.P. ADMINISTRATION — Diane Smith (60,000)
- CLERICAL STAFF — Mark Jacobson (12,500)
- CLERICAL STAFF — Debbie Ebrite (12,500)
- WAREHOUSE MANAGER — Claude White (25,000)
  - INVENTORY MANAGER — Harry Golden (20,000)
  - WAREHOUSE STAFF — Wilma Hannig (15,000)
  - WAREHOUSE STAFF — Penny Kluge (12,500)
  - WAREHOUSE STAFF — Arnold Wonder (12,500)

V.P. MARKETING/SALES — Daniel Darrow (60,000)
- CLERICAL STAFF — Kate Allen (12,500)
- CLERICAL STAFF — Betty Johnson (12,500)
- SALESPERSON — Philip McNeil (20,000)
- SALESPERSON — Laura Hansen (20,000)
- SALESPERSON — Emily Shore (20,000)
- SALESPERSON — Dean Harryton (20,000)
- SALESPERSON — Faye Nash (20,000)

SYSTEMS DIRECT DETROIT LOCATION FLOOR PLAN

During your initial visit to Systems Direct, you were taken on a tour of the premises, after which you drew out the following sketch. The new facility outside Chicago is similarly laid out.

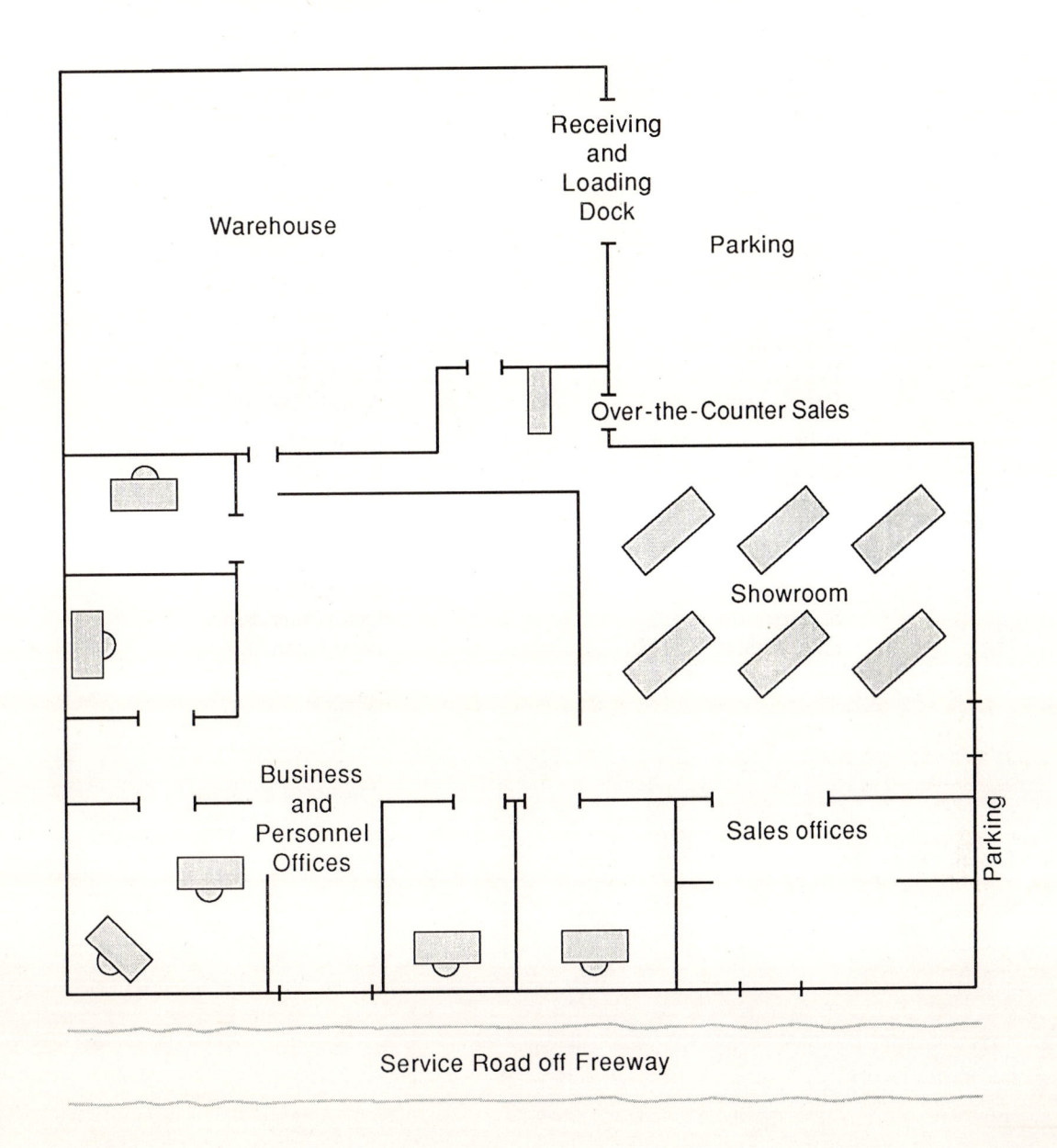

- Warehouse
- Receiving and Loading Dock
- Parking
- Over-the-Counter Sales
- Showroom
- Business and Personnel Offices
- Sales offices
- Parking
- Service Road off Freeway

Permanent File 5

List of Employees

President	Curtis Jackson
Vice-President—Finance	Julie Medina
Chief Accountant	Rosanna Hanna
General Ledger Bookkeeper	Kevin Greenbay
Accounts Receivable Bookkeeper	Wanda Windor
Accounts Payable Bookkeeper	Ben Kato
Clerical Staff	Valerie Vazquez
Clerical Staff	Eric Mitchell
Vice-President—Administration	Diane Smith
Clerical Staff	Mark Jacobson
Clerical Staff	Debbie Ebrite
Warehouse Manager	Claude White
Inventory Manager	Harry Golden
Warehouse Staff	Wilma Hannig
Warehouse Staff	Penny Kluge
Warehouse Staff	Arnold Wonder
Vice-President—Marketing/Sales	Daniel Darrow
Clerical Staff	Kate Allen
Clerical Staff	Betty Johnson
Salesperson	Philip McNeil
Salesperson	Laura Hansen
Salesperson	Emily Shore
Salesperson	Dean Harryton
Salesperson	Faye Nash

Chart of Accounts

Acct Num.	Account Title
100	Petty Cash
101	Cash in Bank—Regular
102	Cash in Bank—Payroll
110	Marketable Securities
120	Accounts Receivable—Equipment
121	Accounts Receivable—Parts and Supplies
122	Notes Receivable—Equipment
123	Discount on Notes Receivable
124	Allowance for Doubtful Accounts
125	Other Receivables
130	Inventories—Equipment
131	Inventories—Parts and Supplies
140	Prepaid Expenses
200	Land
210	Building
211	Accumulated Depreciation—Building
220	Trucks and Cars
221	Accumulated Depreciation—Trucks and Cars
230	Warehouse Equipment
231	Accumulated Depreciation—Warehouse Equipment
240	Office Equipment
241	Accumulated Depreciation—Office Equipment
250	Leases
251	Accumulated Amortization—Leases
300	Accounts Payable—Trade
301	Accounts Payable—Other
310	Current Portion of Long-Term Debt
311	Lease Obligation—Current
312	Pension Obligation
320	Accrued Expenses—Salaries, Interest, Bonuses
330	Payroll Taxes Withheld and Accrued
335	Income Taxes Payable
340	Dividends Payable
350	Deferred Income Taxes
400	Mortgage Payable
410	Notes Payable—Vehicles and Equipment
412	Lease Obligation
500	Capital Stock
510	Additional Paid-In Capital

Acct Num.	Account Title
520	Retained Earnings
521	Dividends Declared
522	Income Summary
600	Sales—Equipment
601	Sales—Parts and Supplies
605	Sales Discounts
610	Sales Returns and Allowances
620	Other Income
626	Interest Income
700	Cost of Sales—Equipment
701	Cost of Sales—Parts and Supplies
705	Purchases Discounts
706	Purchase Returns and Allowances
710	Freight-In on Purchases
800	Salaries and Bonuses—Officers
801	Salaries and Bonuses—Other
802	Employee Benefits (including pensions)
803	Payroll Taxes Expense
805	Advertising and Promotion Expense
806	Bad Debts Expense
807	Delivery Expense (including gas, oil, repairs)
810	Depreciation Expense—Building
811	Depreciation Expense—Trucks and Cars
812	Depreciation Expense—Warehouse Equipment
813	Depreciation Expense—Office Equipment
814	Amortization Expense—Leases
815	Insurance Expense
816	Interest Expense
817	Miscellaneous Expense
818	Office Supplies Expense
819	Professional Services
820	Repairs and Maintenance Expense
821	Taxes and Licenses Expense (excluding payroll taxes)
822	Telephone Expense
823	Travel and Entertainment Expense
824	Utilities Expense (heat, light, water)
825	Gain/Loss—Disposal of Fixed Assets
827	Loss on Obsolete Inventory
830	Income Tax Expense

Minutes of Meetings of
Board of Directors/Stockholder

December 15, 1987:
   Approved salaries for 1988.
   Approved bonuses for 1987 after reviewing the financial statements for November, 1987 and the eleven months then ended; bonus computations to be based on twelve-month figures.
   Reappointed Dewitt and Tanner, CPAs, as independent auditors for 1988.
   Reappointed Brown and Beaver, Attorneys, to serve as general counsel for a quarterly retainer fee of $2,500.
   Declared annual dividend of $100 per share payable January 10, 1988, to holders of record December 31, 1987.

April 15, 1988:
   Reviewed 1987 annual report with audited financial statements.
   Nothing else of audit significance.

July 15, 1988:
   Nothing of audit significance.

October 15, 1988:
   Nothing of audit significance.

December 15, 1988:
   Approved salaries for 1989 including a 10% increase across the board.
   Approved bonuses for 1988 based on a review of financial statements for November and the eleven months then ended; bonus computations to be based on twelve-month figures.
   Reappointed Dewitt and Tanner, CPAs, to 1989 audit. There was some discussion as to whether the auditors were sufficiently able to handle our demands for increasing information on a timely basis, especially as we grow and diversify our product lines into computers and related equipment.
   Reappointed Brown and Beaver, Attorneys, for next year and approved the quarterly retainer fee of $2,500.
   Declared annual dividend of $100 per share payable January 15, 1989, to holders of record December 31, 1988.

April 15, 1989:
   Reviewed 1988 annual report.
   Discussed the need to have a warehouse in the Chicago area to serve the expanding market and to reduce delivery costs. After some discussion, the board authorized the Vice-President - Finance and the Vice-President - Marketing/Sales to explore available sites in the Chicago area.

October 15, 1989:
   Approved the appointment of Smith and Weiss, CPAs, to succeed Dewitt and Tanner, CPAs, beginning with the 1990 audit. This early appointment will allow the new firm to be present at the inventory to be taken at the end of the year.

December 15, 1989:
   Approved salaries for 1990 as per organizational chart in the permanent file.
   Approved the following bonuses for 1989:

President - 10% of income <u>after</u> all other bonuses and
<u>after</u> income taxes.
Vice-President - Marketing/Sales - 10% of income <u>before</u>
income taxes, but <u>after</u> salespersons' bonuses.
5 Salespersons - 20% of excess over quota.

Declared annual dividend of $100 per share payable January 10, 1990, to holders of record on December 31, 1989.

Approved reappointment of Brown and Beaver, Attorneys, to serve as general counsel for a quarterly retainer fee of $2,500.

April 15, 1990:

Reviewed 1989 annual report. Expressed need to upgrade computer processing of data and transactions. The Vice-President - Marketing/Sales indicated the need for more timely sales data. This is necessary to prepare purchase orders for inventory replacement, add new products, drop slow-moving items, etc. It was agreed that Smith and Weiss would undertake a management consulting assignment after the 1990 audit is completed. The purpose of the assignment is to identify areas where additional computerization would prove beneficial, select the appropriate equipment and software, and train Systems Direct personnel in its use. Another purpose of the management consulting assignment is to recommend methods and procedures to improve internal administrative and accounting controls.

October 1, 1990:

At this special meeting the Board authorized the lease agreement for a warehouse and office space with Chicago Properties, Ltd. The property is located off Interstate 80 south of Chicago. This location should expand the company's market area and also reduce delivery expenses. Details of the lease agreement are in the permanent file.

October 15, 1990:

In order to finance the expansion of operations into the Chicago area, the board authorized the president and the vice-president of finance to enter into a ten-year loan agreement with Chicago Suburban Bank. Under the agreement, the bank will provide working capital as needed up to a maximum of one million dollars, with interest at 1/4% above the prime rate. The company agrees to maintain a compensating cash balance of $100,000 and further agrees to the following:
- Officers' salaries are limited to an annual increase of not more than 10%.
- Dividend payments may not exceed net income after taxes during the term of the note.

(The loan agreement was signed October 18, 1990, but no money was advanced as of December 31, 1990. In January, however, the company will borrow $500,000 to finance initial inventory and other assets necessary to begin operations in Chicago in early 1991.)

December 15, 1990:

Approved salaries for 1991 reflecting a 10% increase across the board.
Approved 1990 bonuses as follows:
President - 10% of net income after all bonuses and
<u>after</u> income taxes.
Vice-President - Marketing/Sales - 10% of income <u>before</u> income
taxes, but <u>after</u> salespersons' bonuses.
Salespersons - 20% of sales in excess of quota, before
audit adjustments.

Approved hiring two additional salespersons to cover new areas served by the Chicago location.

Declared annual dividend of $100 per share payable January 15, 1991, to holders of record on December 31, 1990.

Lease Agreement

<u>Landlord</u>:
Chicago Properties, Ltd.

<u>Tenant</u>:
Systems Direct

<u>Property</u>:
Building in South Chicago Industrial Park, off Interstate 80.

<u>Term of Occupancy</u>:
October 1, 1990 to September 30, 2010.

<u>Renewal Option</u>:
Tenant has the option to renew for another twenty-year period at a rent to be negotiated.

<u>Purchase Option</u>:
Tenant has an option to purchase the property at any time for a price equal to its fair market value, as determined by reference to the assessed value.

<u>Monthly Rental</u>:
$6,000 payable in advance. First payment due October 1, 1990, with $6,000 payable the first of each month thereafter.

<u>Other</u>:
All utilities and occupancy costs to be paid by tenant.
All partitions, interior modifications, etc., revert to the landlord at termination of the lease.

<u>Note</u>: This is deemed to be a capital lease. Systems Direct's cost of capital is 12%.

DeWitt and Tanner
Certified Public Accountants
4 Main Street
Detroit, Michigan

REPORT OF CERTIFIED PUBLIC ACCOUNTANTS

The Board of Directors and Stockholders
Systems Direct

We have audited the balance sheets of Systems Direct as of December 31, 1989 and 1988, and the related statements of income, retained earnings and cash flows for the two years then ended. These financial statements are the responsibility of the Company's management; our responsibility is to express an opinion on these financial statements based on our audit.

We conducted our audit in accordance with generally accepted auditing standards. Those standards require that we plan and perform the audit to obtain reasonable assurance about whether the financial statements are free of material misstatement. An audit examines on a test basis, evidence supporting the amounts and disclosures in the financial statements. An audit also includes assessing the accounting principles used and significant estimates made by management, as well as evaluating the overall financial statement presentation. We believe that our audit provides a reasonable basis for our opinion.

In our opinion, the financial statements referred to above present fairly, in all material respects, the financial position of Systems Direct, as of December 31, 1989 and 1988, and the results of its operations and changes in its financial position for the years then ended in conformity with generally accepted accounting principles.

DeWitt and Tanner
Certified Public Accountants

February 28, 1990

Permanent File

Balance Sheet   File name: prybs
December 31, 1989 and 1988   Cells used: a1.c 70

	1989	1988
Assets		
Current assets:		
Cash on hand and in banks	$242,495	$231,500
Accounts receivable	810,050	597,150
Allowance for doubtful accounts	(43,480)	(36,440)
Inventories	384,475	324,821
Prepaid expenses	8,400	5,400
Total current assets	$1,401,940	$1,122,431
Plant, property, and equipment:		
Land	$50,000	$50,000
Building	1,250,000	1,250,000
Accumulated depreciation	(100,000)	(75,000)
Truck and cars	136,000	126,000
Accumulated depreciation	(107,562)	(86,125)
Warehouse equipment	20,000	20,000
Accumulated depreciation	(10,000)	(7,500)
Office equipment	64,500	63,500
Accumulated depreciation	(39,000)	(26,100)
Total plant, prop., & equip.	$1,263,938	$1,314,775
Total assets	$2,665,878	$2,437,206
Liabilities and Stockholders' Equity		
Current liabilities:		
Accounts payable - trade	$478,832	$414,477
Accounts payable - other	12,800	9,350
Mortgage payable - current portion	8,279	7,495
Employee benefits payable	14,280	12,850
Salaries, bonuses, interest - accrued	71,954	52,925
Payroll taxes withheld & accrued	9,394	9,420
Income taxes payable	40,006	30,015
Dividends payable	100,000	100,000
Total current liabilities	$735,545	$636,532
Long-term liabilities:		
Mortgage payable	$974,021	$981,516
Less current portion	(8,279)	(7,495)
Total long-term liabilities	$965,742	$974,021
Total liabilities	$1,701,287	$1,610,553
Stockholders' equity:		
Capital stock (par value $100; authorized, 10,000 shares; outstanding, 1,000 shares)	$100,000	$100,000
Additional paid-in capital	250,000	250,000
Retained earnings	614,591	476,653
Total stockholders' equity	$964,591	$826,653
Total liability and stockholder's equity	$2,665,878	$2,437,206

The accompanying notes to financial statements are an integral part of this statement.

Systems Direct
Income Statements
For Years Ended December 31, 1989 and 1988

File name: pryis
Cells used: a1.e76

	1989		1988	
Sales		$6,521,150		$5,539,970
Less: Sales discounts	$130,400		$109,300	
Sales ret. and allow	65,200	195,600	54,600	163,900
Net sales		$6,325,550		$5,376,070
Cost of sales:				
Beginning inventory	$324,821		$251,146	
Purchases			4,493,626	3,825,390
Freight-in			130,280	109,237
Available for sale	$4,948,727		$4,185,773	
Less: Ending inventory	384,475	4,564,252	324,821	3,860,952
Gross profit		$1,761,298		$1,515,118
Other revenue:				
Other income			3,260	2,730
Income before oper. exp.		$1,764,558		$1,517,848
Operating expenses:				
Salaries - officers	$277,654		$229,700	
Salaries - other	357,900		335,525	
Employee benefits	92,479		76,850	
Payroll taxes expense	44,621		36,900	
Advertising & promotion	32,610		27,330	
Bad debts expense	92,600		81,980	
Delivery expense	57,310		43,700	
Depreciation expense:				
Building	25,000		25,000	
Trucks and cars	28,937		41,625	
Warehouse equipment	2,500		2,500	
Office equipment	12,900		12,700	
Insurance expense	24,120		20,220	
Interest expense	97,814		99,170	
Miscellaneous expense	19,883		16,400	
Office supplies expense	7,226		5,465	
Professional services	31,090		34,430	
Repairs and maintenance	19,780		8,200	
Taxes and licenses exp.	61,730		60,120	
Telephone expense	36,080		21,860	
Travel & entertainment	16,410		13,665	
Utilities expense	29,350	1,367,994	24,600	1,217,940
Income before income taxes		$396,564		$299,908
Less: Income tax expense		158,626		119,963
Net income		$237,938		$179,945

The accompanying notes to financial statements are an integral part of this statement.

Systems Direct
Statements of Retained Earnings
For Years Ended December 31, 1989 and 1988

	1989	1988
Beginning balance	$476,653	$396,708
Add net income	237,938	179,945
	$714,591	$576,653
Less dividends	100,000	100,000
Ending balance	$614,591	$476,653

The accompanying notes to financial statements are an integral part of this statement.

Systems Direct   File name: cashflow
Statements of Cash Flows   Cells used: a1.h32
Years Ended December 31, 1989 and 1988

	Year Ended December 31	
	1989	1988
Cash flows from operating activities:		
Net income, per income statement	$237,938	$179,945
Add: Depreciation	69,337	81,825
Increase in current liabilities (other than long-term debt)	98,229	75,500
Increase-deferred income taxes	0	0
	$405,504	$337,270
Less: Increase in current assets (other than cash)	268,514	178,486
Net cash flow - operating activities	$136,990	$158,784
Cash flows from investing activities:		
Cash paid for purchase of equipment	(18,500)	(77,500)
Cash flows from financing activities:		
Cash paid on long-term debt $ 7,495		$ 6,784
Cash paid for dividends 100,000	(107,495)	100,000 (106,784)
Increase in cash	$ 10,995	$(25,500)
Cash - Beginning of year	231,500	257,000
Cash - End of year	$242,495	$231,500

The accompanying notes to financial statements are an integral part of this statement.

Notes to Financial Statements

1. Summary of accounting policies

Inventory valuation. Inventories are valued at the lower of cost or market, as determined by the first-in, first-out (FIFO) method.

Fixed assets and depreciation. Plant, property, and equipment are stated at cost and depreciated over their estimated useful lives. Trucks and automobiles are depreciated using the double-declining balance method. All other fixed assets are depreciated on the straight-line method. Policy of the company is to take a full year's depreciation in the year of acquisition and no depreciation in the year of disposal.

Income taxes. The provision for income taxes is based on pre-tax income reported in the income statement regardless of the period when such items are reported for tax purposes. The effective income tax rate for 1990 was 40%.

2. Mortgage payable. First mortgage note is held by the Suburban Bank of Detroit and is secured by a lien on the land and building. The mortgage carries an interest rate of 10% and monthly payments of $8776 for a period of thirty years, beginning January 1, 1986.

Engagement Letter

SMITH & WEISS
Certified Public Accountants

93 Third Street
Detroit, Michigan

October 23, 1989

Systems Direct
Detroit, Michigan

Dear Mr. Jackson:

This will confirm our understanding of the arrangements for our examination of the financial statements of Systems Direct for the year ended December 31, 1990.

We will examine the company's balance sheet at December 31, 1990, and the related statements of income, retained earnings, and statement of cash flows for the year then ended, for the purpose of expressing an opinion on them. Our examination will be made in accordance with generally accepted auditing standards and, accordingly, will include such tests of the accounting records and such other auditing procedures as we consider neces- sary in the circumstances.

Our procedures will include tests of documentary evidence supporting the transactions recorded in the accounts, tests of the physical existence of inventories, and direct confirmation of receivables and certain other assets and liabilities by correspondence with selected customers, creditors, legal counsel, and banks. At the conclusion of our examination, we will request certain written representations from management about the financial statements and related matters.

Our engagement is subject to the inherent risk that material errors, irregularities, or illegal acts, including fraud or defalcations, if they exist, will not be detected. However, we will inform you of any such matters that come to our attention.

We will review the company's federal and state income tax returns for the fiscal year ended December 31, 1990. These returns, we understand, will be prepared by the financial vice-president.

Further, we will be available during the year to consult with you on the tax effects of any proposed transactions or contemplated change in business policies.
Our fee for these services will be at our regular per diem rates, plus travel and other out-of-pocket costs. Invoices will be rendered every two weeks and are payable on presentation.

We are pleased to have this opportunity to serve you.
If this letter correctly expresses your understanding, please sign the enclosed copy where indicated and return it to us.

Very truly yours,

Smith and Weiss, CPAs

Arrangements accepted:

C. Jackson   10/28/89
President   Date

Systems Direct

Source: Ricchiute, David N. *Auditing.* 2nd ed. Cincinnati: South-Western Publishing Co., 1988.

Permanent File 17

WORKING TRIAL BALANCE

Systems Direct
Working Trial Balance
December 31, 1990

File name: trialbal
Cells used: a1.k144

Acct. Num.	Account Title	W/P REF.	Per Audit 12/31/89	Per Client 12/31/90	Adjustments Dr.	Cr.	Income Statement Dr. (Cr.)	Balance Sheet Dr. (Cr.)
100	Petty cash		300	300				
101	Cash in bank - Regular		242,195	358,300				
102	Cash in bank - Payroll			0				
110	Marketable securities							
120	Accts. receivable - Equipment		608,550	650,290				
121	Accts.receivable - Parts and suppl.		201,500	105,476				
122	Notes Receivable - Equipment			140,780				
123	Discount on notes receivable							
124	Allow. for doubtful accounts		(43,480)	(52,020)				
125	Other receivables							
130	Inventories - Equipment		374,205	575,525				
131	Inventories - Parts and supplies		10,270	15,373				
140	Prepaid expenses		8,400	45,750				
200	Land		50,000	50,000				
210	Building		1,250,000	1,250,000				
211	Accum. depreciation - Building		(100,000)	(122,913)				
220	Trucks and cars		136,000	173,000				
221	Accum. dep'n. - Trucks and cars		(107,562)	(110,525)				
230	Warehouse equipment		20,000	20,000				
231	Accum. dep'n. - Warehouse equipment		(10,000)	(12,288)				
240	Office equipment		64,500	67,000				
241	Accum. dep'n. - office equipment		(39,000)	(50,825)				
250	Leases			18,000				
251	Accum. amortization - Leases							
300	Accounts payable - Trade		(478,832)	(487,519)				
301	Accounts payable - Other		(12,800)	(3,300)				
310	Current portion - Mortgage Payable		(8,279)	0				
311	Current portion - Lease Obligation							
312	Pension obligation		(14,280)	(15,908)				
320	Accrued Expenses - Sal.,int., bonuses		(71,954)	(132,579)				
330	Payroll taxes withheld and accrued		(9,394)	(13,306)				
335	Income taxes payable		(40,006)	(47,026)				
340	Dividends payable		(100,000)	(100,000)				
350	Deferred income taxes							
400	Mortgage payable		(965,742)	(965,742)				
410	Notes payable - Vehicles & equipment							
412	Lease obligation - Long-term							

Permanent File

500	Capital stock	(100,000)	(100,000)
510	Additional paid-in capital	(250,000)	(250,000)
520	Retained earnings	(476,653)	(614,591)
521	Dividends declared	100,000	100,000
522	Income summary		
600	Sales - Equipment	(4,891,900)	(5,731,585)
601	Sales - Parts and supplies	(1,629,250)	(2,137,637)
605	Sales discounts	130,400	155,800
610	Sales returns and allowances	65,200	77,900
620	Other income - sales of packing crates	(3,260)	(3,903)
626	Interest income		
700	Cost of sales - Equipment	3,697,047	4,307,531
701	Cost of sales - Parts and supplies	736,925	978,111
705	Purchase discounts		
706	Purchase returns and allowances		
710	Freight in on purchases	130,280	155,800
800	Salaries and bonuses - Officers	277,654	291,000
801	Salaries and bonuses - Other	357,900	431,015
802	Employee benefits - incl. pensions	92,479	103,793
803	Payroll tax expense	44,621	50,146
805	Advertising and promotion	32,610	39,020
806	Bad debt expense	92,600	99,000
807	Delivery expenses - Gas, oil, repairs	57,310	62,400
810	Depreciation expense - Building	25,000	22,913
811	Depreciation expense - Trucks and cars	28,937	26,400
812	Depreciation expense - Warehouse eqpt.	2,500	2,288
813	Depreciation expense - Office eqpt.	12,900	11,825
814	Amortization expense - Lease		
815	Insurance expense	24,120	22,000
816	Interest expense	97,814	97,030
817	Miscellaneous expense	19,883	23,410
818	Office supplies expense	7,226	12,003
819	Professional services	31,090	28,600
820	Repairs and maintenance	19,780	18,750
821	Taxes and licenses	61,730	66,000
822	Telephone expense	36,080	41,212
823	Travel and entertainment	16,410	17,510
824	Utilities - Heat, light and water	29,350	31,827
825	Gains/Loss - Sale of fixed assets		1,563
827	Loss on obsolete inventory		
830	Income tax expense	158,626	207,026
	Totals	0	0

Permanent File 19

RECURRING MONTHLY GENERAL JOURNAL ENTRIES

To facilitate the preparation of monthly income statements, Systems Direct prepares a series of general journal entries based on estimates for selected expenses for the following year. These are recorded monthly during the year to estimate the selected expenses for the interim monthly statements. The amounts of the monthly accruals for bonuses and income taxes vary since they are based on monthly income statements. Because of the timely availability of the year-end statements, the client did not post the December recurring entries, nor did they prepare financial statements for the month of December.

As part of your audit, Systems Direct requests that you provide them with similar estimated amounts to be used in preparing the 1991 monthly entries, based on 1990 actual expenses.

```
Systems Direct                                  File name:   rgj90
Recurring Monthly General Journal Entries       Cells used:  a1.d38
For 1990

Acct.
No.    Accounts                                 Debit        Credit
-----  ---------------------------------------  -------      -------
Depreciation expenses:
 810   Building                                 2,083
 211       Accum. Depr. - Building                           2,083
 811   Trucks and Cars                          2,400
 221       Accum. Depr. - Trucks and Cars                    2,400
 812   Warehouse Equipment                        208
 231       Accum. Depr. - Warehouse Equipment                  208
 813   Office Equipment                         1,075
 241       Accum. Depr. - Office Equipment                   1,075
 250   Lease
 251       Accum. Amortization - Lease


 806   Bad Debt Expense                         9,000
 121       Allowance for Doubtful Accounts                   9,000

 815   Insurance Expense                        2,000
 140       Prepaid Expense                                   2,000

 800   Salaries and Bonuses - Officers          Various
 801   Salaries and Bonuses - Other             Various
 320       Accrued Expenses                                  Various

 819   Professional Expenses                    2,600
 140       Prepaid Expenses                                  2,600

 822   Taxes and Licenses                       6,000
 140       Prepaid Expenses                                  6,000

 830   Income Tax Expense                       Various
 335       Income Tax Payable                                Various
```

ASSIGNMENT 1

GENERAL MATTERS

AUDIT PROGRAM

Pre-Fieldwork Procedures

Initials   Date

1. Review correspondence files, prior years' audit working papers, permanent files, financial statements, and auditor's reports. *DJ* ____
2. Coordinate the assistance of entity personnel in data preparation. PBC schedules. *DHW* ____
3. Establish the timing of the audit work. *DHW* ____
4. Establish and coordinate staffing requirements. *DHW* ____
5. Arrange with the client for such matters as adequate working space for the auditors and access to records. *DHW* ____
6. Prepare or update a written audit program. (In practice, sections of the program may be pre-pared or updated at various times during the audit.) *DHW* ____
7. Comply with company policy on engagement letters. *DHW* ____

Fieldwork

Initials   Date

1. Meet client personnel, tour facilities, and draw a diagram of the facilities for permanent file. *DHW* ____
2. Update permanent file. *DHW* ____
3. Interview Systems Direct personnel to become familiar with operating procedures. From your notes, prepare a description of the essential operating procedures. *DHW* ____
4. [↑ system] From the narrative of operating procedures, prepare flowcharts as the procedures exist and the documents flow at the present time. ____ ____
5. [all systems] Prepare a list of internal control weaknesses which you have observed by reviewing the narrative and your flowcharts. ____ ____

Required:

1. Complete the audit program.
2. Turn in the following in the order listed:
    a. Time budget
    b. Audit program *pg 343*
    c. Flowcharts *316*
    d. List of internal control weaknesses

4. Pick out ↑ system & flowchart

Time budget

21

The following is a form of time budget used in public accounting as a basis for charging staff time to clients. Students should keep a record of time spent on each phase of the audit (to the nearest 1/4 hour), and submit these time budgets with each assignment so the instructor may record accumulated time spent on the audit.

```
        SMITH AND WEISS, CPAs    File name:      timebud
               Time Budget       Cells used:     a1.k34
                      CLIENT: Systems Direct
           STAFF ACCOUNTANT: ENTER YOUR NAME
                HOURLY RATE: ENTER YOUR G.P.A. x $ 20
                         H O U R S   W O R K E D   D A I L Y      TOTAL    TOTAL
         ASSIGNMENTS     SUN  MON  TUES  WED  THURS  FRI  SAT     HOURS   CHARGES

  1  Review permanent file                                         0.00     0.00
     Prepare flow charts                                           0.00     0.00
     Perform analytical review                                     0.00     0.00
                                                                   0.00     0.00
  2  Cash                                                          0.00     0.00
                                                                   0.00     0.00
  3  Receivables-Revenue                                           0.00     0.00
                                                                   0.00     0.00
  4  Inventory-Payables                                            0.00     0.00
                                                                   0.00     0.00
  5  Other Current Assets                                          0.00     0.00
                                                                   0.00     0.00
  6  Plant,Property and Equipment                                  0.00     0.00
                                                                   0.00     0.00
  7  Other Current Liabilities                                     0.00     0.00
                                                                   0.00     0.00
  8  Long-term Liabilities                                         0.00     0.00
                                                                   0.00     0.00
  9  Stockholders' Equity                                          0.00     0.00
                                                                   0.00     0.00
 10  Completing the Audit                                          0.00     0.00
                                                                  -----    -----
                 Totals                                            0.00     0.00
```

Note: Use Lotus function to suppress zeros in range that includes total hours and total charges.

These descriptions are your notes from interviews with Systems Direct personnel, and are to be used in preparing flowcharts of the document progression through the accounting and information systems. You should read through the entire narrative of operating procedures and then insert your initials and the date on #4 of the fieldwork portion of the audit program.

Prepare the flowcharts from your notes, using the headings suggested below. As you proceed, indicate weaknesses in the system. These weaknesses will be incorporated in the management letter you will write at the conclusion of the audit. Numbers in brackets [ ] are provided as clues in identifying control weaknesses.

Systems Direct may engage your firm to recommend ways of strengthening the controls so that greater reliance may be placed on these controls in the future. Therefore your supervisor has asked that you also make preliminary notes of ways to strengthen the controls. Check with your instructor for a specific assignment.

As you proceed to flowchart the operations and note weaknesses in the system, you should keep in mind the basic internal control concepts regarding segregation of the following duties:

    Authorization—of transactions
    Custody of assets—a treasury function
    Recording transactions—controllership, chief accountant
    Periodic accountability—independent verification

The following headings serve as a guide in preparing the flowcharts:

    Office—Customer Orders
    Order Filling
        Customer Orders
        Driver
        Over the Counter
    Vice-President—Marketing/Sales
    Inventory Control
    Warehouse—Receiving
    Accounts Receivable—Billing
    Office—Cash Receipts
    Accounts Payable—Bookkeeper
    Vice-President—Finance
        Cash Disbursements
        Payroll

NARRATIVE OF OPERATING PROCEDURES

Processing Customers' Orders

Upon receipt of a customer's order, either by mail or by telephone, any one of four clerks prepares a pre-numbered four-part sales order.

The following description is the procedure for equipment orders and orders including equipment, parts, and supplies. Only orders for parts and supplies are routinely processed without credit approval.

The entire four-part sales order form is sent to the Vice-President—Marketing/Sales for credit approval. [1] Credit is rarely denied since Systems Direct knows most of its retail outlet customers. Slow-paying customers are notified that payment in full must accompany their orders or the orders will be shipped COD. Initial orders from new accounts have been "cleared" through the salesperson making the initial contact with the new customer. This has resulted in occasional bad debt write-offs in the past. The number of write-offs has been increasing recently.

After initialing approval of the customer's order, copies 1, 2, and 3 of the sales order are returned to the business office. Copy 4 remains with marketing and sales for sales analysis and is then filed by customer account. Copy 1 is sent to the customer confirming the order. [2] Copy 2 is sent to the warehouse to prepare the shipment. Copy 3 is sent to the accounts receivable bookkeeper for billing and posting to the accounts receivable subsidiary ledger. [3]

It was noted that customers are sometimes billed for back-ordered items not in stock. This has caused some confusion in posting customers' accounts, since customers do not include back-ordered items in their remittances.

Sales returns of equipment, parts, and supplies are delivered to the warehouse, where any available warehouse employee prepares a list of items returned and notes the customer's name thereon. A copy is made and given (or sent) to the customer as a receipt, while the original is used to update the inventory. The original is then sent to the accounts receivable bookkeeper to credit the customer's account.

Over-the-counter sales of parts and supplies are made to customers in the area who wish to save delivery time. Any available warehouse employee takes and fills their orders at the parts and supplies counter. Customers pay either by check or cash, or

Assignment 1   23

charge the purchase to their accounts. In the latter case, charge tickets are prepared that are periodically delivered to the accounts receivable clerk. Cash and checks are periodically delivered to the office to be included with the bank deposit for that day, after being recorded as sales.

Warehouse and Shipping

Warehouse receives copy 2 of the sales order from the office and fills the order as promptly as possible. Promptness depends on the availability of the merchandise and of delivery trucks. Equipment orders are sometimes held pending receipt of other orders from the same general delivery area so as to minimize delivery expenses. Parts and supplies orders are generally shipped by United Parcel Service. Items not in stock are noted on the sales order as "not in stock." [4]

The person filling the order makes two copies of the sales order, [5] which then become shipping order copies 1 and 2. Copy 2 of the sales order is then sent to accounts receivable. The accounting bookkeepers are instructed only to bill for items shipped. Sometimes, however, the bookkeepers fail to note back-ordered items, and the customer is billed for the entire order.

Both copies of the shipping order accompany the delivery driver. Upon delivery of the order to the customer, the driver has the customer initial copy 1 of the shipping order as a receipt. The driver returns this copy to the inventory clerk in the warehouse. The customer retains the second copy of the shipping order. In the case of UPS shipments, one copy is sent to the customer along with the merchandise. The second copy is returned to the inventory clerk in the warehouse and serves as a receipt.

Inventory Control—Warehouse

A perpetual inventory system is maintained for equipment and computer software only. Upon receipt of the initialed copy of the shipping order, the inventory is reduced by the quantity of the equipment delivered. [6]

After adjusting the perpetual inventory records, the initialed shipping order copy is sent to the accounts receivable bookkeeper for filing by customer account.

When a stock item is low, or reaches a predetermined minimum level, an inventory clerk informally notifies the Vice-President—Marketing/Sales. This notification may be verbal or a handwritten note left with someone in marketing and sales. [7]

The Vice-President—Marketing/Sales decides whether to reorder the item or to order a newer or different model. The Vice-President—Marketing/Sales also determines the quantity to order. [8]

Purchase order copy 2 is received from the Vice-President—Marketing/Sales and temporarily filed alphabetically by vendor pending receipt of the merchandise. When the merchandise arrives, a warehouse employee compares the purchase order copy 2 with the packing slip accompanying the merchandise. If correct, the employee initials the purchase order copy 2 which is now, in effect, a receiving report. It is then sent to the inventory manager for updating the perpetual inventory records. The inventory manager then sends both the initialed purchase order copy 2 and the packing slip to the accounts payable bookkeeper.

Purchase returns are rare. Defective equipment is usually handled as an allowance to the amount owed and the charge to purchases is reduced accordingly.

Vice President—Marketing/Sales

The Vice-President—Marketing/Sales receives a four-part sales order from the clerk preparing the customer's order. After credit approval, he returns copies 1, 2, and 3 to the office and retains copy 4.

Copy 4 is retained for sales analysis by one of the clerks. This analysis is done periodically on manually prepared spreadsheets. The spreadsheet shows sales by customer, by salesperson, by area and city, and by product. [9]

Purchase orders for new or replacement equipment are prepared on a three-part pre-numbered purchase order form by a sales department clerk upon direction of the Vice-President—Marketing/Sales. Copy 1 is sent to the vendor, copy 2 is sent to the warehouse, and copy 3 is temporarily filed in marketing by vendor, pending receipt of the vendor's invoice. [10]

Upon receipt of the vendor's invoice, purchase order copy 2 and the vendor's invoice are compared for quantities and arithmetic accuracy before the vendor's invoice is sent to the accounts payable bookkeeper. [10] [11] [12]

Accounts Payable Bookkeeper

The accounts payable bookkeeper also compares the vendor's invoice with the initialed copy of the purchase order and the packing slip received from the warehouse. [10]

1. Office - customer orders should keep a copy of the sales order in their office. Credit approval should be said from outside of Marketing/Sales maybe V.P. Finance.

2. Confirming an order before checking to see that all supplies ordered are in stock and ready for shipment.

3. Recording transaction before knowing that all goods being billed for have been shipped. Should be done after sales order goes to shipping.

4. A sales invoice should be made out with the description & quantities of goods sold, the price including freight, insurance, terms & other relevant data so as not to be confusing to the accounts receivable clerk.

5. There should be sufficient copies of shipping order made so one can be kept in the warehouse records. Also, should be verified & approved.

6. Inventory clerk should not make out shipping orders & also be able to reduce inventory levels.

7. The authorized inventory clerk should fill out a purchase requisition which should go to the warehouse manager.

8. The company should have a policy that tells what the quantity is to be ordered.

9. Should also include quantity & price if a complete sales analysis is being done.

10.

He then prepares a three-part check and remittance advice; that is, an original and two copies, and sends these together with all attachments to the Vice-President—Finance. [13]

A voucher register is not used since invoices are generally paid on a timely basis, taking advantage of the discount terms.

Vice-President—Finance

After receiving the "package" from accounts payable, the Vice-President—Finance examines the underlying documentation, and if in order, signs the check and mails it to the vendor. A clerk then prepares a check summary [14] and files copy 3 of the check numerically by check number.

The check summary is prepared in two parts. One copy is sent to the chief accountant; the other copy is retained in a chronological file to be used to reconcile the bank statement.

The remaining documents (i.e., vendor's invoice, initialed purchase order copy, packing slip, and copy 2 of the check and remittance advice) are returned to accounts payable for filing by vendor account. [15]

Accounts Receivable Bookkeeper

Upon receipt of copy 3 of the sales order, the accounts receivable bookkeeper compares it to copy 2 received from the warehouse after the order has been filled and shipped. It was previously noted that customers were sometimes billed for back-ordered items.

The accounts receivable bookkeeper prepares a three-part sales invoice. [16] Copy 1 is mailed to the customer and copy 2 is sent to marketing/sales. Copy 3 is used to prepare the sales journal and to post the customers' accounts in the subsidiary ledger. [17] Copy 3 is then filed in the customer's file folder.

The sales journal (summary) is sent to the general ledger bookkeeper for posting to the general ledger accounts.

Cash Receipts

The majority of customers mail their payments by invoice. Monthly statements are sent only to those customers who have past due balances. The only cash sales made are to local customers who come directly to the warehouse for parts and supplies. (See description for over-the-counter sales under Processing Customers' Orders.) Since cash sales are incidental and represent less then five percent of all parts and supplies sales, these sales are handled quite informally.

The cash in the till from over-the-counter sales is not deposited daily, but is left to accumulate until the amount warrants deposit. Usually deposits are made one to three times weekly depending on the time of year and amount of sales. When deemed sufficient, the cash is given to the person making the deposit that day and is included with the regular deposit, being noted as "cash sales." [18]

Any of the warehouse personnel, depending upon availability, serve the over-the-counter customer. [19]

Sales of parts and supplies are not subject to perpetual inventory procedures, and consequently, there is no perpetual control over this portion of the inventory. (Cost/benefit must obviously be considered in any recommendation in this area.)

For monthly statement purposes, the parts and supplies inventory is estimated by the gross profit method. For convenience, the chief accountant uses a uniform gross profit rate; however, the actual gross profit of many parts and supplies varies. Prices of parts and supplies are adjusted once a year. The last management letter called attention to significant year-end adjustments to the parts and supplies inventory.

Incoming mail from customers generally includes checks and remittance advices. Any available person in the office opens the mail, rubber stamps the checks with the company's restrictive "For deposit only" endorsement, and lists the checks on a two-part List of Receipts form. [20]

Copy 1 of the list of receipts, along with the checks, is given to the person making the bank deposit. This may be any one of several employees in the office, depending on availability and convenience, since the deposit is usually made on the person's lunch hour. Afternoon mail receipts are held in the company safe until the following day, when they are deposited with that morning's cash receipts. [21]

Copy 2 of the list of receipts, along with the customers' remittance advices and other correspondence, is sent to the accounts receivable bookkeeper for posting to the customer's accounts in the subsidiary ledger. Remittance advices are filed in the customers' files, as is the correspondence after proper review and handling. [22]

The accounts receivable bookkeeper also prepares the cash receipts journal from the list of checks. Upon completion, she sends the list of checks to the

Assignment 1   25

Vice-President—Finance and sends the cash receipts journal to the general ledger bookkeeper. [23]

The Vice-President—Finance receives and reconciles the monthly bank statements. She also receives a copy of the check register against which to match the cancelled checks.

Payroll

Because of the small number of employees and the informal atmosphere, internal control over payroll has not been a concern.

Annual salaries for the next year are established by the company officers/directors at the last board meeting of the year. The Vice-President—Administration maintains personnel records and sends to the Vice-President—Finance a time report for the period. Absences, overtime, vacations, and other notations that affect the payroll appear on this time report. This document is used in preparing the payroll journal, payroll voucher, and payroll checks.

The Vice-President—Finance prepares both the biweekly and the monthly payrolls. Officers are paid monthly whereas all other employees are paid biweekly. A separate payroll checking account is maintained. Each pay period, a check from the regular checking account, representing the net payroll for the period, is deposited in the payroll checking account.

After preparing the payroll, the Vice-President—Finance gives the payroll voucher summarizing the payroll to the general ledger bookkeeper.

The Vice-President—Finance signs both regular checks and payroll checks and reconciles both checking accounts. [23] Due to other matters demanding her attention, she occasionally falls behind and has to reconcile several months' bank statements at a time.

When she is out of town, regular checks awaiting her signature lie on her desk pending her return. When she anticipates being out of town, she sometimes signs several checks in advance so as not to delay the procedure. Her secretary safeguards these checks and performs her duties as described above before mailing the checks to vendors. Signatures on payroll checks are affixed by a check writer with a signature stamp.

Accounting and Monthly Financial Statement Procedures

Wanda Windor maintains the accounts receivable subsidiary file and provides Julie Medina, the Vice-President—Finance, an aging every month showing accounts both current and past due. Since most customers pay by invoice, she sends monthly statements only to customers who have past due balances.

Ben Kato is in charge of maintaining purchases and accounts payable and provides monthly to Rosanna Hanna, the chief accountant, a list of unpaid invoices and purchase commitments.

The chief accountant, Rosanna Hanna, prepares the monthly financial statements as well as periodic budgetary reports. She is also responsible for filing the various local, state, and federal tax returns.

The following financial statements and reports are prepared monthly:

- Balance sheet
- Income statement—in comparison with prior year as well as current year's budget
- Cash flow statement
- List of accounts receivable
- List of accounts payable

There is no evidence of periodic comparison of perpetual inventory records with the physical equipment, parts, and supplies.

There is no evidence to suggest that anyone accounts for missing pre-numbered documents and forms.

Note: As discussed earlier, while you are flowcharting the operations and noting weaknesses in the system, you should keep in mind the basic internal control concepts regarding segregation of the following duties:

Authorization of transactions

Custody of assets—a treasury function

Recording transactions—controllership, chief accountant

Periodic accountability—independent verification

You should also focus on the control points where errors may occur. Thus pay attention to manual operations with respect to both inputs and outputs (independent verification). Also, each department initiating a document should keep a copy of such document in its files; either in numerical or chronological order, whichever is appropriate.

ASSIGNMENT 2

PETTY CASH AND REGULAR AND PAYROLL CASH ACCOUNTS

AUDIT PROGRAM

Summary of assignment:

Complete petty cash workpaper.
Prepare interbank transfer schedule.
Verify reconciliation of both bank accounts.
Prepare bank cutoff analysis.
Prepare necessary adjusting entries.
Complete lead schedule.

General

	Initial	Date

1. Foot and crossfoot lead schedule and all other PBC schedules, i.e., bank reconciliation. ____ ____

2. Compare balances on other PBC schedules with balances on lead schedules. ____ ____

3. Compare balances on lead schedules with account balances in the trial balance. ____ ____

Analytical Review Procedures

1. Review entries to general ledger cash accounts and investigate unusual (including General Journal) entries to Petty Cash, Cash in Bank—Regular, and Cash in Bank—Payroll accounts. *DHW* ____

2. Review monthly bank reconciliations of Cash in Bank—Regular and Cash in Bank—Payroll accounts. *DHW* ____

Other Substantive Procedures (Year-End)

Petty Cash

1. Count petty cash, complete schedule, and have petty cash custodian sign workpapers at conclusion of count. *DHW* ____

2. Complete petty cash workpaper and prepare adjusting entry, if necessary. ____ ____

Cash in Bank—Regular and Payroll

3. Obtain bank confirmations at year-end and cutoff bank statements as of January 8, 1991. *DHW* ____

4. List all items on bank cutoff statements and trace to cash receipts and the check register, noting differences. See partially completed schedule in workpapers. ____ ____

5. Prepare a schedule of interbank transfers for December and verify proper recording of interbank transfers. See partially completed schedule in workpapers. ____ ____

Cash in Bank—Regular

6. Verify correctness of Bank reconciliation by:

   a. Tracing the deposit(s) to both the cash receipts journal and the bank cutoff statement ____ ____

   b. Comparing outstanding checks with entries in the check register and with those returned by the bank with the cutoff statement ____ ____

   c. Preparing adjusting entry, if necessary ____ ____

Cash in Bank—Payroll

7. Verify clerical accuracy of selected payrolls:

   a. Several during the year *DHW* ____

   b. December 30, 1990 ____ ____

8. Verify accuracy of payroll deductions with personnel records. *DHW* ____

9. Trace net payroll to check register:

   a. Several during the year *DHW* ____

   b. December 31, 1990 ____ ____

10. Verify correctness of bank reconciliation by:

    a. Tracing deposits in transit, if any, to the check register and to the bank cutoff statement ____ ____

    b. Comparing December 30 net payroll to charges on the payroll

27

	Initial	Date
bank account cutoff statement to determine that all payroll checks cleared the bank. (Canceled payroll checks not included with bank cutoff statement.)	___	___
c. Preparing adjusting entry, if necessary	___	___

Cash—All accounts

11. Review for proper financial statement disclosure and classification—noting restrictions on cash, if any.   *DHW*   ___

Reminder to students:

The following procedure should be followed with adjusting entries:

a. Write out in detail with complete explanation on or after the schedule(s) to which they pertain,

b. and in the AJE file in numerical order.

c. Summarize in the appropriate supporting schedules and in the lead schedule, and

d. post to the working trial balance.

Required:

1. Complete the audit program.
2. Turn in the following in the order listed:

   a. Time budget

   b. Audit program with your initials and date work was performed

   c. Cash lead schedule (File name: CASH-LEAD)

   d. List of adjusting journal entries with complete explanations

   e. Petty cash worksheet (File name: PETTY-CAS)

   f. Bank reconciliations: Regular account (File name: BANKREC) Payroll account (File name: BANKRECP)

   g. Bank cutoff analysis—Regular account (File name: CUTANLY)

   h. Interbank transfer schedule

```
Systems Direct                          File name:   cashlead
Cash Lead Schedule (PBC)                Cells used:  a1.h36
December 31, 1990


Acct.                          Trial      Adjustments              Per
No.    Account Title           Balance  #   Dr.    #   Cr.         Audit
-----  -------------------     -------  --  -----  --  -------     ----------

 100   Petty Cash                  300

 101   Cash - Regular          358,300




 102   Cash - Payroll                0
                               --------     --------    --------    --------
       Totals                   358,600
                               ========     ========    ========    ========

Audit adjustments:
```

Systems Direct   File name: pettycas
Petty Cash   Cells used: a1.d53

Counted December 30, 1990, in the presence of
Eric Mitchell, petty cash custodian.

	Denomination	Quantity	Total Amount
Bills:	------------	--------	------
	$10	4	
	5	12	
	1	23	
Coins:	$0.50	3	
	0.25	16	
	0.10	22	
	0.05	12	
	0.01	15	
Stamps:	0.25	17	

Total currency and stamps

Receipts:
  Postage stamps $68.00
  Coffee, sugar, etc., for office   12.30
  COD receipt for parts delivery   12.75
  Receipt for items for office Xmas tree   20.80
  I.O.U. Daniel Darrow   25.00
  Gas ticket - Julie Medina travel expenses   15.00

    Totals

Returned to me intact *E. Mitchell*

Note: round entries to nearest dollar.

Totals
Shortage

Balance per trial balance - Imprest amount
AJE 1

Balance per audit
                                                  =======
Audit Adjustment:

Assignment 2   29

```
Systems Direct                        File name:    bankrec
Bank Reconciliation (PBC)             Cells used:   a1.f48
Regular Account
December 31, 1990


Bank Balance - December 31, 1990                            417,300
Deposits in transit:                         13,980
                                             33,570          47,550
                                           --------        --------
    Total                                                  464,850

Checks Outstanding:       Ck. No.    Date      Amount
                         --------  --------  --------
ABC, Inc.                 89925    12/20/89       325
HI-FI Corp                89942    12/23/89       650
Telephone Co.             90917    12/15/90     2,750
Hewlett-Hudson            90930    12/27/90    32,575
Pear Computer Co.         90931    12/27/90    23,500
Analog Computers          90932    12/27/90    28,750
GreenCross/Shield         90934    12/28/90     5,500
City of Detroit           90935    12/29/90    12,500    106,550
                                              --------  --------
Balance per trial balance                                358,300

Audit adjustments:




                                              --------  --------
Balance per audit
                                                        ========



Comments:
```

30   Assignment 2

```
Systems Direct                          File name:      bankrecp
Bank Reconciliation                     Cells used:     a1.f55
Payroll Account (PBC)
December 31, 1990


Bank balance - December 31, 1990                                        0
Deposit in transit                                                 30,564
                                                                  --------
Balance per ledger (Cash in Bank - Payroll)                        30,564

Outstanding checks:
                                    Deductions
         Employee     Ck. No.  Gross    (20%)       Net
         --------     -------  -----  ----------  -------
    C. Jackson         1201    6,250    1,250      5,000
    J. Medina          1202    5,000    1,000      4,000
    D. Smith           1203    5,000    1,000      4,000
    D. Darrow          1204    5,000    1,000      4,000
    R. Hanna           1205    3,333      667      2,666
    C. White           1206    2,084      417      1,667
    K. Greenbay        1207      963      193        770
    W. Windor          1208      674      135        539
    B. Kato            1209      674      135        539
    V. Vazquez         1210      576      115        461
    E. Mitchell        1211      576      115        461
    M. Jacobson        1212      481       96        385
    D. Ebrite          1213      481       96        385
    H. Golden          1214      769      154        615
    W. Hannig          1215      576      115        461
    P. Kluge           1216      481       96        385
    A. Wonder          1217      481       96        385
    K. Allen           1218      481       96        385
    B. Johnson         1219      481       96        385
    P. McNeil          1220      769      154        615
    L. Hansen          1221      769      154        615
    E. Shore           1222      769      154        615
    D. Harryton        1223      769      154        615
    F. Nash            1224      769      154        615
                              -------  -------    -------
         Totals                38,205    7,641     30,564     30,564
                              =======  =======    =======   --------

Balance per audit                                                       0
                                                                  ========
Audit adjustment:
```

STANDARD BANK CONFIRMATION INQUIRY
Approved 1966 by
AMERICAN INSTITUTE OF CERTIFIED PUBLIC ACCOUNTANTS
and
BANK ADMINISTRATION INSTITUTE (FORMERLY NABAC)

ORIGINAL
To be mailed to accountant

January 4, 19 91

Your completion of the following report will be sincerely appreciated. IF THE ANSWER TO ANY ITEM IS "NONE," PLEASE SO STATE. Kindly mail it in the enclosed stamped, addressed envelope *direct* to the accountant named below.

Report from

Yours truly,

Systems Direct
(ACCOUNT NAME PER BANK RECORDS)

(Bank) Suburban National Bank

Detroit, Michigan

By *Julie Medera*
Authorized Signature

Bank customer should check here if confirmation of bank balances only (item 1) is desired. ☐

NOTE—If the space provided is inadequate, please enter totals hereon and attach a statement giving full details as called for by the columnar headings below.

Accountant Smith and Weiss, CPAs

1. At the close of business on December 31, 19 90 our records showed the following balance(s) to the credit of the above named customer. In the event that we could readily ascertain whether there were any balances to the credit of the customer not designated in this request, the appropriate information is given below.

AMOUNT	ACCOUNT NAME	ACCOUNT NUMBER	Subject to Withdrawal by Check?	Interest Bearing? Give Rate
$ 417,300	Checking	07240-2830	yes	none
0	Payroll	07240-2831	yes	none

2. The customer was directly liable to use in respect of loans, acceptances, etc., at the close of business on that date in the total amount of $ 965,742.00 as follows:

AMOUNT	DATE OF LOAN OR DISCOUNT	DUE DATE	INTEREST Rate	INTEREST Paid to	DESCRIPTION OF LIABILITY, COLLATERAL, SECURITY INTERESTS, LIENS, ENDORSERS, ETC.
$ 965,742.00	1/1/1986	MONTHLY	10%	12/31/90	Mortgage note secured by property occupied by Systems Direct

3. The customer was contingently liable as endorser of notes discounted and/or as guarantor at the close of business on that date in the total amount of $ _____ as below:

AMOUNT	NAME OF MAKER	DATE OF NOTE	DUE DATE	REMARKS
$				

4. Other direct or contingent liabilities, open letters of credit, and relative collateral, were

_____

5. Security agreements under the Uniform Commercial Code or any other agreements providing for restrictions, not noted above, were as follows (if officially recorded, indicate date and office in which filed):

_____

Yours truly, (Bank) Suburban National Bank

Date January 10, 19 91 By *Wendy Perrin*
Authorized Signature

Additional copies of this form can be obtained from the American Institute of CPAS, 1211 Avenue of the Americas, New York, NY 10036-8775

Assignment 2

Systems Direct
Interbank Transfers
December 31, 1990

File name: intbank
Cells used: a1.h21

From Regular Account: To Payroll Account:

Date	Ck. No.	Amount		Date	Amount	Comment
12/4	90901	30,735		12/5	30,735	
12/18	90922	30,705		12/19	30,705	

1/2/91   1/2/91

Comment:

Assignment 2   33

Systems Direct
December 30, 1990 Payroll (PBC)
December 31, 1990

File name: payroll
Cells used: a1.g50

Employee	Ck. No.	Gross	Deductions (20%)	Net
C. Jackson	1201	6,250	1,250	5,000
J. Medina	1202	5,000	1,000	4,000
D. Smith	1203	5,000	1,000	4,000
D. Darrow	1204	5,000	1,000	4,000
R. Hanna	1205	3,333	667	2,666
C. White	1206	2,084	417	1,667
K. Greenbay	1207	963	193	770
W. Windor	1208	674	135	539
B. Kato	1209	674	135	539
V. Vazquez	1210	576	115	461
E. Mitchell	1211	576	115	461
M. Jacobson	1212	481	96	385
D. Ebrite	1213	481	96	385
H. Golden	1214	769	154	615
W. Hannig	1215	576	115	461
P. Kluge	1216	481	96	385
A. Wonder	1217	481	96	385
K. Allen	1218	481	96	385
B. Johnson	1219	481	96	385
P. McNeil	1220	769	154	615
L. Hansen	1221	769	154	615
E. Shore	1222	769	154	615
D. Harryton	1223	769	154	615
F. Nash	1224	769	154	615
Totals		38,205	7,641	30,564

Audit memos:
General journal entry made by client to record payroll was dated December 30, 1990, and was inspected by DHW.

800 Salaries and Bonuses - Officers	21,250	
801 Salaries and Bonuses - Other	16,955	
802 Employee Benefits	3,821	
803 Payroll Taxes Expense	1,273	
320 Accrued Expenses - Payroll		30,564
312 Pension Obligations		3,821
331 Payroll Taxes W/H and Accrued		8,914

Note: Payroll checks were distributed to employees on 12-30-90.

Selected Cash Receipts
1990 and 1991

Date	Source of Receipt	Account Number	Amount Received	Deposit
12-20	B. and G. Electronics	122	$ 3,500	
	Appliance T.V., Inc	120	8,450	
	Three Star Stereo	120	12,220	
	Albion Sounds	120	2,430	
12-21	Stereo Supermarket	120	5,600	
	Travis Electronics	120	13,560	$45,760
12-22	King Systems	120	$16,400	
12-23	A. & B. Computers	122	1,500	
	Panorama Stereo	120		6,750
	Cash sales	601	870	25,520
12-26	Scheerens Stereo	120	$ 4,325	
	Alma Computers	120	12,870	
	Comptech Corp	120	12,110	
12-28	Macroland	120	8,020	
	Cash sales	601	420	37,745
12-29	Allen Stereos	120	$ 5,670	
	Quadrophonics	120	3,990	
	Fortune Sound Center	120	4,320	13,980
12-31	PC, Unlimited	120	$ 500	
	Diskway Corp.	20	1,200	
	Columbus Computer Land	122	3,120	
	Chicago Stereo	120	7,100	
	Ohio Ultra Sound	120	8,850	
	Indiana Electronics, Inc.	600	12,800	33,570
1-4-89	ABEL Computers, Inc.	120	$ 4,675	
	Harmony Music Shop	20	1,575	
	Cash sales - Dec. 30	601	1,925	8,175
1-5	Alpha-Beta, Inc.	120	$ 7,244	
	Anderson Electronics	120	8,519	15,763
1-6	Mercury Music Shop, Ltd.	120	$ 3,988	
	Travis Tech Center	120	6,607	10,595
1-7	Electric Sound Center	120	$ 1,926	
	Uptown Computers, Inc.	120	4,849	
	Sunny Sounds, Unlimited	120	6,469	
	Albion Sounds	120	4,411	17,655
1-8	Suburbanville Computers	120	$ 2,006	
	Tapedeck Center	120	8,245	10,251

Check Register - Selected Sections
December, 1990 and January, 1991

Date	Check #	Payee		Amount	Acct
12-04-90	90900	Suburban Nat'l Bank (Nov. mort. pmt.)		$ 8,776	400
	90901	Cash -		30,735	102
	90902	Petty Cash Custodian		235	Variable
	90903	Universal Freight		1,430	710
	90904	Chicago Properties		6,000	250
	90905	Detroit Electric Co		3,340	824
12-08-90	90906	IMA, Inc.		42,000	700
	90907	Xenio Corp.		32,000	700
	90908	RSC, Inc.		33,000	700
	90909	Panorama Electronics		40,575	700
	90910	Speakers, Ltd.		30,500	700
	90911	Turntables, Inc.		32,500	700
	90912	Cambridge Word Processing, Inc		22,000	700
12-15-90	90913	Atachi, Inc.		13,000	700
	90914	Games, Unlimited		30,750	700
	90915	San Jose Software, Ltd.		12,500	700
	90916	I.R.S. - 4th qtr. income tax estimate		40,000	335
	90917	Telephone Co.		2,750	822
12-18-90	90918	Truck Supply Co.		3,700	807
	90919	Void		0	
	90920	Red City Office Supply Co		2,320	818
	90921	Auto Fuel, Inc.		1,750	807
	90922	Cash - Payroll		30,705	102
12-20-90	90923	BDBO Advertising, Inc.		12,500	805
	90924	Petty Cash Custodian		275	Variable
	90925	Void		0	
	90926	Michigan Florists		25	817
	90927	Wholesalers Trade Journal		50	805
12-27-90	90928	Wong Computers		35,000	700
	90929	Digitel, Inc.		19,100	700
	90930	Hewlett Hudson Co.		32,575	700
	90931	Pear Computer Co.		23,500	700
	90932	Analog Computers		28,750	700
	90933	Suburban Nat'l Bank - Dec. mort. pmt		8,776	400
12-28-90	90934	Green Cross/Shield		5,500	802
	90935	City of Detroit - 1/2 '91 R.E. tax bil		12,500	140
1-02-91	90936	Cash - Payroll	Dec.31	30,564	102
	91100	Chicago Properties - lease pmt.		6,000	210
	91101	Building Repairs, Inc	Dec	3,300	301
	91102	Void		0	
	91103	Janitorial Service	Dec.	250	820
	91104	Truck Supply, Inc	Dec	1,840	807
	91105	Xenio Corp.	Dec	17,450	300
	91106	Universal Freight	Dec	1,550	710
	91107	Turntables, Inc.	Dec	23,060	300
	91108	Red City Office Supply	Dec	375	818
	91109	Auto Fuel, Inc.	Dec.	1,680	807
	91110	4 Star Restaurant	Jan.	72	823
	91111	Detroit Electric Co.	Dec.	3,750	824
	91112	Telephone Co.	Dec.	2,300	822

	91113	Brown and Beaver, Attnys - 4th qtr. '90		2,500	140
	91114	Trash Removal Service	Dec.	300	820
1-05-91	91115	Pear Computer Company	Dec.	22,660	300
	91116	Cambridge Word Processors	Dec.	12,000	300
	91117	IMA, Inc.	Dec.	31,778	300
	91118	Wong Computers, Inc.	Dec.	33,050	300
	91119	Analog Computer Corp.	Dec.	40,050	300
	91120	Hewlett Hudson	Dec.	20,500	300
	91121	NAC Printer Mfg. Co.	Dec.	9,180	300
	91122	Speakers, Ltd.	Dec.	21,780	300
	91123	Mobile Computer Mfg. Co.	Dec.	18,870	300
	91124	Panorama Electronics, Inc.	Dec.	71,820	300
	91125	RSC, Inc.	Dec.	29,458	300
	91126	Digitel, Inc.	Dec.	31,500	300
	91127	San Jose Software, Inc.	Dec.	17,300	300
	91128	Games, Inc.	Dec.	11,910	300
	91129	Unicorn Mfg. Co.	Dec.	23,875	300
1-06-91	91130	Pension Trustee	Dec.	15,908	312
	91131	I. R. S. - PR tax	Dec.	13,306	330

Note: January checks in payment of December invoices are indicated by **Dec.**

Suburban National Bank
Cutoff Bank Statement - Regular Account
January 8, 1991

Date	Check #	Amount	Deposits		Balance
12-31-90					$417,300
1-02-91	90936	$30,564	$13,980		400,716
1-05-91	90930	32,575	15,370	20,975	404,486
1-06-91	90932	28,750	15,763		
	Counter check	300			391,199
1-07-91	91101	3,300	10,595		
	90931	23,500			374,994
1-08-91	90935	12,500	17,655		
	91103	250			
	91104	1,840			
	91108	375			
	91110	72			
	91934	5,500			
	91100	6,000			366,112

Suburban National Bank
Cutoff Bank Statement - Payroll Account

Date	Check #	Amount	Check #	Amount	Deposits	Balance
12-31-90						
1-02-91	1205	$2,666	1224	$ 615	$30,564	$ 0
	1216	385	1212	385		
	1201	5,000	1207	770		
	1222	615	1209	539		
	1202	4,000	1206	1,667		13,922
1-03-91	1210	461	1215	461		
	1223	615	1220	615		
	1214	615	1203	4,000		
	1221	615	1204	4,000		2,540
1-04-91	1219	385	1213	385		
	1208	539				1,231
1-05-91	1211	461	1217	385		
	1218	385				0

Note: Deposit ticket and cancelled checks are not included with payroll account cutoff statement. You may assume that they agree with the entries on the cutoff statement.

38   Assignment 2

Systems Direct
Bank Cutoff Analysis
Regular Account
December 31, 1990

File name: cutanly
Cells used: a1.h54

Checks - Cutoff Statement

Date	Ck. No.	Amount
1-4-91	90936	30,564
1-5-91	90930	32,575
1-6-91	90932	28,750
	C. Check	300
1-7-91	91101	3,300
	90931	23,500
1-8-91	90935	12,500
	91103	250
	91104	1,840
	91108	375
	91110	72
	90934	5,500
	91100	6,000

Check Register

Date Recorded	Amount	Differences and Comments

Deposits - Cutoff Statement

Date	Amount	Amount
1-4-91	5,670	
	3,990	
	4,320	13,980
1-5-91	1,925	
	12,800	
	4,675	
	1,575	20,975
1-5-91	3,120	
	1,700	
	8,850	
	1,700	15,370
1-6-91	7,244	
	8,519	15,763
1-6-91	3,988	
	6,607	10,595
1-8-91	1,926	
	4,849	
	6,469	
	4,411	17,655
		94,338
		94,338
		======

Deposits - Cash Receipts

Date	Amount	Amount	Differences
		0	
		0	
		======	

Assignment 2

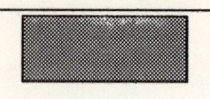

Deposit Ticket 1

SYSTEMS DIRECT
123 State Street
Detroit, Michigan

DATE January 4, 1991

SUBURBAN NATIONAL BANK
Detroit, Michigan

Acct. # 07240 2830

12-3456/7890

CURRENCY		
COIN		
CHECKS	Allen Stereos	5,670.00
	Quadrophonics	3,990.00
Total from other side		4,320.00
TOTAL		13,980.00

Deposit Ticket 2

SYSTEMS DIRECT
123 State Street
Detroit, Michigan

DATE January 5, 1991

SUBURBAN NATIONAL BANK
Detroit, Michigan

Acct. # 07240 2830

12-3456/7890

CURRENCY		1,925.00
COIN		
CHECKS	Indiana Electronics	12,800.00
	Abel Computers	4,675.00
	Harmony Music	1,575.00
Total from other side		
TOTAL		20,975.00

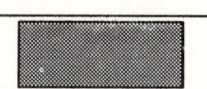

Deposit Ticket 3

SYSTEMS DIRECT
123 State Street
Detroit, Michigan

DATE January 5, 1991

SUBURBAN NATIONAL BANK
Detroit, Michigan

Acct. # 07240 2830

12-3456/7890

CURRENCY		
COIN		
CHECKS	Columbus Computer - Note	3,120.00
	Chicago Stereo	1,700.00
	Ohio Ultra Sound	8,850.00
Total from other side		1,700.00
TOTAL		15,370.00

Deposit Ticket 4

SYSTEMS DIRECT
123 State Street
Detroit, Michigan

DATE January 6, 1991

SUBURBAN NATIONAL BANK
Detroit, Michigan

Acct. # 07240 2830

12-3456/7890

CURRENCY		
COIN		
CHECKS	Alpha-Beta, Inc.	7,244.00
	Anderson Electric	8,519.00
Total from other side		
TOTAL		15,763.00

SYSTEMS DIRECT
123 State Street
Detroit, Michigan

DEPOSIT TICKET

12–3456/7890

DATE January 7 19 91

SUBURBAN NATIONAL BANK
Detroit, Michigan

Acct. # 07240 2830

CURRENCY		
COIN		
CHECKS	Mercury Micro	3,988.00
	Travis Tech.	6,607.00
Total from other side		
TOTAL		10,595.00

SYSTEMS DIRECT
123 State Street
Detroit, Michigan

DEPOSIT TICKET

12–3456/7890

DATE January 8 19 91

SUBURBAN NATIONAL BANK
Detroit, Michigan

Acct. # 07240 2830

CURRENCY		
COIN		
CHECKS	Electric Sound	1,926.00
	Uptown Computers	4,849.00
	Sunny Sounds	6,469.00
	Albion Sounds	4,411.00
Total from other side		
TOTAL		17,655.00

SYSTEMS DIRECT
123 State Street
Detroit, Michigan

Check No. 90936
Date 12-30-90

12–3456/7890

Pay to the order of CASH - PAYROLL $ 30,564.00

THIRTY THOUSAND FIVE HUNDRED SIXTY-FOUR AND NO/100-------------------- DOLLARS

Memo: December 30 Payroll

FOR SIMULATION ONLY

J. Medina
P. Kato

SUBURBAN NATIONAL BANK
Detroit, Michigan
Acct. # 07240 2830

Assignment 2

SYSTEMS DIRECT
123 State Street
Detroit, Michigan

Check No. 90930
Date 12-22-90
12–3456/7890

Pay to the order of HEWLETT-HUDSON CO. $ 32,575.00

THIRTY-TWO THOUSAND FIVE HUNDRED SEVENTY-FIVE AND NO/100------------ DOLLARS

Memo: December invoice

FOR SIMULATION ONLY

J. Medina
B. Kato

SUBURBAN NATIONAL BANK
Detroit, Michigan
Acct. # 07240 2830

SYSTEMS DIRECT
123 State Street
Detroit, Michigan

Check No. 90932
Date 12-27-90
12–3456/7890

Pay to the order of ANALOG COMPUTERS $ 28,750.00

TWENTY-EIGHT THOUSAND SEVEN HUNDRED FIFTY AND NO/100--------------- DOLLARS

Memo: December invoice

FOR SIMULATION ONLY

J. Medina
B. Kato

SUBURBAN NATIONAL BANK
Detroit, Michigan
Acct. # 07240 2830

COUNTER CHECK

Date 12-27-90

Pay to the order of CURTIS JACKSON $ 300.00

THREE HUNDRED AND NO/100--- DOLLARS

Curtis Jackson

SYSTEMS DIRECT
DETROIT, MICHIGAN

Memo: Travel advance

SYSTEMS DIRECT
123 State Street
Detroit, Michigan

Check No. 91901
Date 1-2-91
12-3456/7890

Pay to the order of   BUILDING REPAIRS, INC. $ 3,300.00

THREE THOUSAND THREE HUNDRED AND NO/100--------------------------------- DOLLARS

Memo: Painting offices Nov. & Dec.

FOR SIMULATION ONLY

J. Medina
B. Kato

SUBURBAN NATIONAL BANK
Detroit, Michigan
Acct. # 07240 2830

SYSTEMS DIRECT
123 State Street
Detroit, Michigan

Check No. 90931
Date 12-27-90
12-3456/7890

Pay to the order of   PEAR COMPUTER CO. $ 23,500.00

TWENTY-THREE THOUSAND FIVE HUNDRED AND NO/100------------------------- DOLLARS

Memo: December invoice

FOR SIMULATION ONLY

J. Medina
B. Kato

SUBURBAN NATIONAL BANK
Detroit, Michigan
Acct. # 07240 2830

SYSTEMS DIRECT
123 State Street
Detroit, Michigan

Check No. 90935
Date 12-28-90
12-3456/7890

Pay to the order of   CITY OF DETROIT $ 12,500.00

TWELVE THOUSAND FIVE HUNDRED AND NO/100--------------------------------- DOLLARS

Memo: 1/2 1991 Real Estate Tax

FOR SIMULATION ONLY

J. Medina
B. Kato

SUBURBAN NATIONAL BANK
Detroit, Michigan
Acct. # 07240 2830

SYSTEMS DIRECT
123 State Street
Detroit, Michigan

Check No. 91103
Date 1-2-91

12–3456/7890

Pay to the order of __JANITORIAL SERVICE__ $ __250.00__

__TWO HUNDRED FIFTY AND NO/100------------------------------------__ DOLLARS

Memo: __December invoice__

FOR SIMULATION ONLY

J. Medina
B. Kato

SUBURBAN NATIONAL BANK
Detroit, Michigan
Acct. # 07240 2830

SYSTEMS DIRECT
123 State Street
Detroit, Michigan

Check No. 91104
Date 1-2-91

12–3456/7890

Pay to the order of __TRUCK SUPPLY, INC.__ $ __1,840.00__

__ONE THOUSAND EIGHT HUNDRED FORTY AND NO/100-----------------------__ DOLLARS

Memo: __December invoice__

FOR SIMULATION ONLY

J. Medina
B. Kato

SUBURBAN NATIONAL BANK
Detroit, Michigan
Acct. # 07240 2830

SYSTEMS DIRECT
123 State Street
Detroit, Michigan

Check No. 91108
Date 1-2-91

12–3456/7890

Pay to the order of __RED CITY OFFICE SUPPLY__ $ __375.00__

__THREE HUNDRED AND SEVENTY-FIVE AND NO/100--------------------------__ DOLLARS

Memo: __December invoice__

FOR SIMULATION ONLY

J. Medina
B. Kato

SUBURBAN NATIONAL BANK
Detroit, Michigan
Acct. # 07240 2830

SYSTEMS DIRECT
123 State Street
Detroit, Michigan

Check No. 91110
Date 1-2-91

12–3456/7890

Pay to the order of   4-STAR RESTAURANT $ 72.00

SEVENTY-TWO AND NO/100-- DOLLARS

Memo: Jan. meeting with customer

FOR SIMULATION ONLY

J. Medina
B. Kato

SUBURBAN NATIONAL BANK
Detroit, Michigan
Acct. # 07240 2830

SYSTEMS DIRECT
123 State Street
Detroit, Michigan

Check No. 90934
Date 12-28-90

12–3456/7890

Pay to the order of   GREEN CROSS & SHIELD $ 5,500.00

FIVE THOUSAND FIVE HUNDRED AND NO/100----------------------------- DOLLARS

Memo: December invoice

FOR SIMULATION ONLY

J. Medina
B. Kato

SUBURBAN NATIONAL BANK
Detroit, Michigan
Acct. # 07240 2830

SYSTEMS DIRECT
123 State Street
Detroit, Michigan

Check No. 91100
Date 1-2-91

12–3456/7890

Pay to the order of   CHICAGO PROPERTIES $ 6000.00

SIX THOUSAND AND NO/100--- DOLLARS

Memo: Lease payment for January

FOR SIMULATION ONLY

J. Medina
B. Kato

SUBURBAN NATIONAL BANK
Detroit, Michigan
Acct. # 07240 2830

Assignment 2

REVENUES AND RECEIVABLES

ASSIGNMENT 3

AUDIT PROGRAM

Summary of assignment:

Test sales cutoff.
Test for errors in billing, prices, extensions, and postings.
Review confirmation exceptions; write off uncollectible accounts.
Review January collections of year-end receivables.
Compute discount on installment notes receivable and amortize by the effective interest method.
Compute bad debts expense using an experience ratio.
Compute unrealized gross profit on installment notes for income tax calculation.

General

                                            Initial Date

1. Foot and crossfoot lead schedule and all other PBC schedules, subsidiary ledgers, etc. ____ ____
2. Compare balances on lead schedules with account balances in the trial balance. ____ ____
3. Compare balances on other PBC schedules and subsidiary ledgers with balances on lead schedule. ____ ____

Analytical Review Procedures

1. Note any unusual relationships between current and prior years, including the following: gross sales, returns and allowances, and discounts; receivables, allowance account, and bad debts expense. ____ ____
2. Scan for unusual entries to above accounts. Analyze entries from general journal to these accounts. *DHW* ____

Other Substantive Procedures

1. Sales cutoff procedures to determine that sales and receivables are recorded in the proper period: ____ ____

                                            Initial Date

    a. Review sales invoices in the sales journal for several days before and after the year-end for clerical accuracy, proper pricing, completeness, and proper posting. ____ ____

    b. Compare with shipping records (sales order copy 1). *DHW* ____

    c. Review credit memos issued after year-end for authorization (appropriate initials approving issuance and recording of credit memoranda. ____ ____

2. On a test basis, trace:

    a. Selected customer account balances to aging schedule. *DHW* ____

    b. Selected account balances on aging schedule to subsidiary ledger *DHW* ____

    c. Selected invoices to customer accounts *DHW* ____

    d. Selected cash receipts to customer account *DHW* ____

3. Send negative confirmations to parts and supplies customers. *DHW* ____

4. Review replies with management. (See comments in workpapers.) Prepare necessary adjusting entries, if any. *DHW* ____

5. Send positive confirmations to equipment and soft-ware customers. *DHW* ____

6. Review replies with management. (See comments in workpapers.) Prepare necessary adjusting entries, if any. ____ ____

7. For trade notes receivable:

    a. Examine all notes receivable. *DHW* ____

    b. Trace opening balances from journal to ledger. *DHW* ____

    c. Trace payments from ledger account to cash receipts journal. *DHW* ____

    d. Verify interest income and accruals. ____ ____

      e. Review replies with management. (See comments in workpapers.) Prepare necessary adjusting entries, if any.

      f. Calculate unrealized gross profit for income tax calculation. (See partially completed workpaper.)

8. Analyze the allowance for doubtful accounts, and verify (or compute) the year-end balance.

9. Determine proper financial statement classification, presentation, and disclosure.

10. Compute estimated bad debts expense for 1991 recurring journal entries.

Required:

1. Complete the audit program.
2. Complete the lead schedule.
3. Turn in the following in the order listed:

    a. Time budget

    b. Audit program

    c. Receivables lead schedule

    d. Adjusting journal entries with complete explanations

    e. Partial sales journal with your comments

    f. Accounts receivable—equipment subsidiary ledger showing audit adjustments and balance per audit

    g. Schedule of notes receivable

    h. Notes receivable worksheet

    i. Unrealized gross profit on notes receivable worksheet

    j. Allowance for doubtful accounts file and worksheet showing calculation of experience ratio

Schedule of Selling Prices of Equipment
(stereos, computers, and software)

	Price by Quarters			
Description	1/1	4/1	7/1	10/1
Electronic Sound Systems				
Self-contained units	$800	$800	$850	$850
Turntables	200	225	225	250
Speakers	250	300	300	300
Amplifiers/Receivers	350	350	375	375
AM/FM Radios	250	250	300	300
Computers				
HH-256	$ 900	$ 900	$ 900	$ 900
Pear-320	100	1000	900	900
Analog-512	1800	1800	1500	1500
Digitel-320	1400	1400	1300	1200
Wong-512	500	500	1400	400
IMA-320	1300	1300	1200	1100
Admiral-64	400	400	300	200
Mobile - 512 Portable			500	500
Xenio Laptop Portables				500
NAC Printers	300	300	250	250
Software				
Cambridge Word Processor	$450	$400	$400	$400
San Jose Spreadsheet	375	375	350	350
IMA Data Base Program	00	400	375	375
Games Package	250	250	200	200

Comments:
All parts and supplies are billed at 100% of cost.

There have been no sales of the Admiral-64 computer during the year. Management agrees to write off as obsolete the entire Admiral-64 inventory.

New first quarter prices have not yet been finalized. Continue to use fourth quarter prices until further notice.

Systems Direct
Receivables Lead Schedule (PBC)
December 31, 1990

File name: reclead
Cells used: a1.i42

Acct. No.	Account Title	Per T/B	#	Adjustments Debit	#	Credit	Per Audit
120	Accounts Receivable - Equipment	650,290					
121	Accounts Receivable - Parts and Supplies	105,476					
122	Notes Receivable Equipment	140,780					
123	Discount on Notes Receivable						
124	Allowance for Doubtful Accounts	(52,020)					
125	Other Receivables						
	Totals	844,526					
806	Bad Debts Expense	99,000					

Audit adjustments:

Assignment 3   49

Systems Direct
Partial Sales Journal
1990 and 1991

File name: salesjou
Cells used: a1.j27

Date	Customer	Acct. No.	Inv. No.	Accts. Rec. #120	Delivery Expense #807	Sales Eqpt. #600	Sales P. and S. #601	Sales Ret./Allow. #610	Comments
12/26/90	Wonderful Music	276	112214	8,866	341	8,150	375		
	McNab Computers	378	112215	5,440	140	5,300			
12/27	Downtown Techtronics	325	112216	10,296	396	9,900			
	Alma Computers	375	112217	3,744	144	3,600			
12/28	Maas Electronics	388	112218	6,760	260	6,500			
	Albion Sounds	126	112219	4,411	111	4,300			
	Rainbow Drive	232	112220	(1,560)	(60)			(1,500)	
12/29	Celler Computers	252	112221	8,528	328	8,100	100		
	Ohio Stereo	342	112222	6,032	232	5,700	100		
	Urban Electronics	365	112223	8,944	344	8,600			
12/30	Impute,Inc	138	112224	2,912	112	2,800			
	Transistor Electron.	280	112225	6,968	268	6,700			
1/2/91	Dickens Computers	285	112226	9,048	273	8,700	75		
	King Systems	272	112227	5,705	280	5,425			
	Hi-Tech Center	407	112228	4,368	168	4,200			
1/3	Sounds,Unlimited	189	112229	2,858	158	2,650	50		
	Townsville Electron.	246	112230	(4,264)	(164)			(4,100)	
1/4	U-Dial, Inc.	408	112231	3,328	128	3,100	100		
1/5	Dayton Computers	409	112232	18,876	726	18,150			

50   Assignment 3

Invoice No. 112214

SYSTEMS DIRECT
123 State Street
Detroit, Michigan

INVOICE No. 112214
DATE: 12/26/90

SOLD TO: Acct. #276
Wonderful Music, Inc.
1714 Tuscaloosa Dr.
Detroit, MI 48228

DELIVER TO: Same

Terms: 1/10, n/30, FOB Detroit

QTY. ORDERED	QTY. SHIPPED	DESCRIPTION	UNIT PRICE	TOTAL
14	14	Turntables	$250	$3,500
7	7	Speakers	300	2,100
3	3	Self-contained - 10K	850	2,550

Thank You

TOTAL EQUIPMENT ORDERED: $8,150
PARTS & SUPPLIES SHIPPED: 375
TOTAL MERCHANIDISE SHIPPED: $8,525
DELIVERY EXPENSE: 341
TOTAL INVOICE AMOUNT: $8,866

Invoice No. 112215

SYSTEMS DIRECT
123 State Street
Detroit, Michigan

INVOICE No. 112215
DATE: 12/26/90

SOLD TO: Acct. #378
McNab Computers
216 Cross Rd.
Toledo, OH 43611

DELIVER TO: Same

Terms: 1/10, n/30, FOB Detroit

QTY. ORDERED	QTY. SHIPPED	DESCRIPTION	UNIT PRICE	TOTAL
2	2	Wong-512	$1,400	$2,800
2	2	San Jose Spreadsheet	350	700

Thank You

TOTAL EQUIPMENT ORDERED: $3,500
PARTS & SUPPLIES SHIPPED: 0
TOTAL MERCHANIDISE SHIPPED: $3,500
DELIVERY EXPENSE: 140
TOTAL INVOICE AMOUNT: $3,640

Assignment 3

SYSTEMS DIRECT
123 State Street
Detroit, Michigan

INVOICE
No. 112216

DATE 12/27/90

SOLD TO: Acct. #325
Downtown Techtronics
406 Main St.
Champaign, IL 61821

DELIVER TO: Same

Terms: 1/10, n/30, FOB Detroit

QTY. ORDERED	QTY. SHIPPED	DESCRIPTION	UNIT PRICE	TOTAL
4	4	IMA-320	$1,100	$4,400
4	4	AM/FM Radio - RAD500	300	1,200
3	3	Self-Contained - 10K	850	2,550
2	2	IMA Data Base Program	375	750
5	5	Games Package	200	1,000

TOTAL EQUIPMENT ORDERED $9,900
PARTS & SUPPLIES SHIPPED 0
TOTAL MERCHANDISE SHIPPED $9,900
DELIVERY EXPENSE 396
TOTAL INVOICE AMOUNT $10,296

Thank You

SYSTEMS DIRECT
123 State Street
Detroit, Michigan

INVOICE
No. 112217

DATE 12/27/90

SOLD TO: Acct. #375
Alma Computers
1920 Independent Dr.
Flint, MI 48503

DELIVER TO: Same

Terms: 1/10, n/30, FOB Detroit

QTY. ORDERED	QTY. SHIPPED	DESCRIPTION	UNIT PRICE	TOTAL
1	1	Digitel-320	$1,200	$1,200
1	1	Pear-320	900	900
1	1	IMA-320	1,100	1,100
1	1	Cambridge Word Processor	400	400

TOTAL EQUIPMENT ORDERED $3,600
PARTS & SUPPLIES SHIPPED 0
TOTAL MERCHANDISE SHIPPED $3,600
DELIVERY EXPENSE 144
TOTAL INVOICE AMOUNT $3,744

Thank You

SYSTEMS DIRECT
123 State Street
Detroit, Michigan

INVOICE
No. 112218

DATE 12/28/90

SOLD TO: Acct. #388
Maas Electronics
314 Middle St.
Archbold, OH 43502

DELIVER TO: Same

Terms: 1/10, n/30, FOB Detroit

QTY. ORDERED	QTY. SHIPPED	DESCRIPTION	UNIT PRICE	TOTAL
4	4	HH-256	$900	$3,600
2	2	San Jose Spreadsheet	350	700
4	4	Turntables - TT100	250	1,000
4	4	Speakers - SP86	300	1,200

TOTAL EQUIPMENT ORDERED $6,500
PARTS & SUPPLIES SHIPPED 0
TOTAL MERCHANDISE SHIPPED $6,500
DELIVERY EXPENSE 260
TOTAL INVOICE AMOUNT $6,760

Thank You

SYSTEMS DIRECT
123 State Street
Detroit, Michigan

INVOICE
No. 112219

DATE 12/28/90

SOLD TO: Acct. #126
Albion Sounds
146 Decatur Dr.
Bowling Green, OH 43402

DELIVER TO: Same

Terms: 1/10, n/30, FOB Detroit

QTY. ORDERED	QTY. SHIPPED	DESCRIPTION	UNIT PRICE	TOTAL
4	4	AM/FM Radios - RAD500	$300	$1,200
2	2	Self-Contained - 10K	850	1,700
3	3	Speakers - SP86	300	900
2	2	Turntables - TT100	250	500

TOTAL EQUIPMENT ORDERED $4,300
PARTS & SUPPLIES SHIPPED 0
TOTAL MERCHANDISE SHIPPED $4,300
DELIVERY EXPENSE 111
TOTAL INVOICE AMOUNT $4,411

Thank You

Assignment 3

Invoice No. 112220

SYSTEMS DIRECT
123 State Street
Detroit, Michigan

CREDIT MEMO

INVOICE
No. 112220
DATE 12/28/90

SOLD TO: Acct. #232
Rainbow Drive, Inc.
1002 Gold St.
Goshen, IN 46526

DELIVER TO: Same

Terms: 1/10, n/30, FOB Detroit

QTY. ORDERED	QTY. SHIPPED	DESCRIPTION	UNIT PRICE	TOTAL
1	1	Analog-512	$1,500	$1,500

TOTAL EQUIPMENT ORDERED $1,500
PARTS & SUPPLIES SHIPPED 0
TOTAL MERCHANIDISE SHIPPED $1,500
DELIVERY EXPENSE 60
TOTAL INVOICE AMOUNT $1,560

Thank You

Invoice No. 112221

SYSTEMS DIRECT
123 State Street
Detroit, Michigan

INVOICE
No. 112221
DATE 12/29/90

SOLD TO: Acct. #252
Celler Computers
2424 Crescent Dr.
Fort Wayne, IN 46805

DELIVER TO: Same

Terms: 1/10, n/30, FOB Detroit

QTY. ORDERED	QTY. SHIPPED	DESCRIPTION	UNIT PRICE	TOTAL
3	3	Digitel-320	$1,200	$3,600
5	5	HH-256	900	4,500

TOTAL EQUIPMENT ORDERED $8,100
PARTS & SUPPLIES SHIPPED 100
TOTAL MERCHANIDISE SHIPPED $8,200
DELIVERY EXPENSE 328
TOTAL INVOICE AMOUNT $8,528

Thank You

SYSTEMS DIRECT
123 State Street
Detroit, Michigan

INVOICE
No. 112222

DATE 12/29/90

SOLD TO: Acct. #342
Ohio Stereo
1894 Twelfth St.
Columbus, OH 44223

DELIVER TO: Same

Terms: 1/10, n/30, FOB Detroit

QTY. ORDERED	QTY. SHIPPED	DESCRIPTION	UNIT PRICE	TOTAL
4	4	Speakers - SP86	$300	$1,200
6	6	Amplifier/Receiver	375	2,250
3	3	Turntables - TT100	250	750
5	5	AM/FM Radio - RAD500	300	1,500

TOTAL EQUIPMENT ORDERED $5,700
PARTS & SUPPLIES SHIPPED 100
TOTAL MERCHANDISE SHIPPED $5,800
DELIVERY EXPENSE 232
TOTAL INVOICE AMOUNT $6,032

Thank You

SYSTEMS DIRECT
123 State Street
Detroit, Michigan

INVOICE
No. 112223

DATE 12/29/90

SOLD TO: Acct. #365
Urban Electronics
719 Willow Lane
Arlington Heights, IL 60008

DELIVER TO: Same

Terms: 1/10, n/30, FOB Detroit

QTY. ORDERED	QTY. SHIPPED	DESCRIPTION	UNIT PRICE	TOTAL
2	2	Cambridge Word Processor	$400	$800
8	8	AM/FM Radio - RAD500	300	2,400
1	1	Self-Contained Stereo	850	850
3	3	Pear-320	1,100	3,300
5	5	Turntables - TT100	250	1,250

TOTAL EQUIPMENT ORDERED $8,600
PARTS & SUPPLIES SHIPPED 0
TOTAL MERCHANDISE SHIPPED $8,600
DELIVERY EXPENSE 344
TOTAL INVOICE AMOUNT $8,944

Thank You

Assignment 3

SYSTEMS DIRECT
123 State Street
Detroit, Michigan

INVOICE
No. 112224

DATE 12/30/90

SOLD TO: Acct. #138
Impute, Inc.
166 Industrial St.
Saginaw, MI 48601

DELIVER TO: Same

Terms: 1/10, n/30, FOB Detroit

QTY. ORDERED	QTY. SHIPPED	DESCRIPTION	UNIT PRICE	TOTAL
1	1	HH-256	$ 900	$ 900
1	1	IMA-320	1,100	1,100
2	2	Cambridge Word Processors	400	800

TOTAL EQUIPMENT ORDERED $2,800
PARTS & SUPPLIES SHIPPED 0
TOTAL MERCHANIDISE SHIPPED $2,800
DELIVERY EXPENSE 112
TOTAL INVOICE AMOUNT $2,912

Thank You

SYSTEMS DIRECT
123 State Street
Detroit, Michigan

INVOICE
No. 112225

DATE 12/30/90

SOLD TO: Acct. #280
Transistor Electronics
3822 Jefferson Dr.
Detroit, Mi 48207

DELIVER TO: Same

Terms: 1/10, n/30, FOB Detroit

QTY. ORDERED	QTY. SHIPPED	DESCRIPTION	UNIT PRICE	TOTAL
3	3	Analog-512	$1,500	$4,500
4	4	IMA Data Base Program	375	1,500
2	2	San Jose Spreadsheet	350	700

TOTAL EQUIPMENT ORDERED $6,700
PARTS & SUPPLIES SHIPPED 0
TOTAL MERCHANIDISE SHIPPED $6,700
DELIVERY EXPENSE 268
TOTAL INVOICE AMOUNT $6,968

Thank You

SYSTEMS DIRECT
123 State Street
Detroit, Michigan

INVOICE
No. 112226
DATE 12/29/90

SOLD TO: Acct. #285
Dickens Computers
800 Park Ave.
Troy, OH 45373

DELIVER TO: Same

Terms: 1/10, n/30, FOB Detroit

QTY. ORDERED	QTY. SHIPPED	DESCRIPTION	UNIT PRICE	TOTAL
3	3	Digitel-320	$1,200	$3,600
3	3	Pear-320	900	2,700
1	1	Wong-512	1,400	1,400
2	2	Cambridge Word Processor	400	800
1	1	Games Package	200	200

TOTAL EQUIPMENT ORDERED $8,700
PARTS & SUPPLIES SHIPPED 75
TOTAL MERCHANDISE SHIPPED $8,700
DELIVERY EXPENSE 273
TOTAL INVOICE AMOUNT $9,048

Thank You

SYSTEMS DIRECT
123 State Street
Detroit, Michigan

INVOICE
No. 112227
DATE 12/29/90

SOLD TO: Acct. #272
King Systems
10905 Mall Blvd.
Dayton, OH 45459

DELIVER TO: Same

Terms: 1/10, n/30, FOB Detroit

QTY. ORDERED	QTY. SHIPPED	DESCRIPTION	UNIT PRICE	TOTAL
2	2	Wong-512	$1,400	$2,800
1	1	IMA-320	1,100	1,100
3	3	IMA Data Base Program	375	1,125
1	1	Cambridge Word Processor	400	400

TOTAL EQUIPMENT ORDERED $5,425
PARTS & SUPPLIES SHIPPED 0
TOTAL MERCHANDISE SHIPPED $5,425
DELIVERY EXPENSE 280
TOTAL INVOICE AMOUNT $5,705

Thank You

Assignment 3

SYSTEMS DIRECT
123 State Street
Detroit, Michigan

INVOICE No. 112228

DATE: 12/30/90

SOLD TO: Acct. #407
Hi-Tech Center
4959 Grove Ave.
South Bend, IN 46628

DELIVER TO: Same

Terms: 1/10, n/30, FOB Detroit

QTY. ORDERED	QTY. SHIPPED	DESCRIPTION	UNIT PRICE	TOTAL
1	1	Digitel-320	$1,500	$1,500
5	5	Speakers - SP86	300	1,500
3	3	Turntables - TT100	250	750
1	1	San Jose Spreadsheet	350	350
1	1	Cambridge Word Processor	400	400

TOTAL EQUIPMENT ORDERED $4,200
PARTS & SUPPLIES SHIPPED 0
TOTAL MERCHANDISE SHIPPED $4,200
DELIVERY EXPENSE 168
TOTAL INVOICE AMOUNT $4,368

Thank You

SYSTEMS DIRECT
123 State Street
Detroit, Michigan

INVOICE No. 112229

DATE: 1/3/91

SOLD TO: Acct. #189
Sounds, Unlimited
9682 Mason Ave.
Oak Lawn, IL 60453

DELIVER TO: Same

Terms: 1/10, n/30, FOB Detroit

QTY. ORDERED	QTY. SHIPPED	DESCRIPTION	UNIT PRICE	TOTAL
1	1	Self-Contained - 10K	$850	$850
3	3	Turntables - TT100	250	750
2	2	Amplifier/Receiver	375	750
1	1	AM/FM Radio - RAD500	300	300

TOTAL EQUIPMENT ORDERED $2,650
PARTS & SUPPLIES SHIPPED 50
TOTAL MERCHANDISE SHIPPED $2,700
DELIVERY EXPENSE 158
TOTAL INVOICE AMOUNT $2,858

Thank You

SYSTEMS DIRECT
123 State Street
Detroit, Michigan

CREDIT MEMO

INVOICE
No. 112230

DATE 12/30/90

SOLD TO: Acct. #246
Townsville Electronics
42 Kellogg Ave.
Battle Creek, MI 49017

DELIVER TO: Same

Terms: 1/10, n/30, FOB Detroit

QTY. ORDERED	QTY. SHIPPED	DESCRIPTION	UNIT PRICE	TOTAL
2	2	Digitel-320	$1,200	$2,400
2	2	Self-Contained - 10K	850	1,700

TOTAL EQUIPMENT ORDERED $4,100
PARTS & SUPPLIES SHIPPED 0
TOTAL MERCHANDISE SHIPPED $4,100
DELIVERY EXPENSE 164
TOTAL INVOICE AMOUNT $4,264

Thank You

SYSTEMS DIRECT
123 State Street
Detroit, Michigan

INVOICE
No. 112231

DATE 1/4/91

SOLD TO: Acct. #408
U-Dial, Inc.
62 Oak Hill Circle
Grand Rapids, MI 49505

DELIVER TO: Same

Terms: 1/10, n/30, FOB Detroit

QTY. ORDERED	QTY. SHIPPED	DESCRIPTION	UNIT PRICE	TOTAL
1	1	IMA-320	$1,100	$1,100
2	2	IMA Data Base Program	375	750
1	1	Self-Contained Stereo	850	850
1	1	Cambridge Word Processor	400	400

TOTAL EQUIPMENT ORDERED $3,100
PARTS & SUPPLIES SHIPPED 100
TOTAL MERCHANDISE SHIPPED $3,200
DELIVERY EXPENSE 128
TOTAL INVOICE AMOUNT $3,328

Thank You

Assignment 3

SYSTEMS DIRECT
123 State Street
Detroit, Michigan

INVOICE
No. 112232

DATE 1/5/91

SOLD TO: Acct. #409
Dayton Computers
819 Stockwell Ave.
Dayton, OH 45424

DELIVER TO: Same

Terms: 1/10, n/30, FOB Detroit

QTY. ORDERED	QTY. SHIPPED	DESCRIPTION	UNIT PRICE	TOTAL
4	4	Analog-512	$1,500	$6,000
6	6	HH-256	900	5,400
4	4	Wong-512	1,400	5,600
1	1	Cambridge Word Processor	400	400
2	2	IMA Data Base Program	375	750

TOTAL EQUIPMENT ORDERED $18,150
PARTS & SUPPLIES SHIPPED 0
TOTAL MERCHANDISE SHIPPED $18,150
DELIVERY EXPENSE 726
TOTAL INVOICE AMOUNT $18,876

Thank You

SYSTEMS DIRECT
123 State Street
Detroit, Michigan

INVOICE
No. 112233

DATE 1/4/91

SOLD TO: Indiana Electronics
6000 State St.
Mishawaka, IN 46544

DELIVER TO: Customer picked up

Terms: 1/10, n/30, FOB Detroit

QTY. ORDERED	QTY. SHIPPED	DESCRIPTION	UNIT PRICE	TOTAL
4	4	San Jose Spreadsheet	$350	$1,400
6	6	Cambridge Word Processor	400	2,400
5	5	HH-256	900	4,500
5	5	Pear-320	900	4,500

Paid by check 1/4/91 C.W.

TOTAL EQUIPMENT ORDERED $12,800
PARTS & SUPPLIES SHIPPED 0
TOTAL MERCHANDISE SHIPPED 0
DELIVERY EXPENSE 0
TOTAL INVOICE AMOUNT $12,800

Thank You

```
Systems Direct                             File name:  eqsubled
Accounts Receivable                        Cells used: a1.h122
Equipment Subsidiary Ledger (PBC)
December 31, 1990

                                                     PAST DUE
Acct.
No.    Name                   Balance    Current   Over 30   Over 60   Over 90   Comments
111    Compro,Inc.             6,029      6,029
115    ANP,Inc.                7,284                7,284
118    Advanced Systems        2,154                          2,154
120    Audio Fidelity          4,402      4,402
126    Albion Sounds           4,411      4,411
134    Beta Corp               9,439                          9,439
135    Alpha,Ltd.              6,480      6,480
138    Impute,Inc.             2,912      2,912
141    Spectral Sounds         8,602      1,748    6,854
145    Harmony Music Shop      1,575      1,575
149    Key Largo Studios       9,832      9,832
150    Anderson Electyronics   8,519      8,519
163    L & M Computers         8,563               8,563
164    Techtronics,Ltd.        8,538      8,538
169    Travis Electronics      3,834      3,834
174    Cato Processors           965                           965
177    Corvette Computers     10,192     10,192
185    Galaxy Sounds           7,860      7,860
189    Sounds, Unlimited       4,863               4,863
192    Stereo Supermart        6,034      6,034
195    Computer Supermart      7,603      7,603
202    Alpha-Beta,Inc.         7,244      7,244
208    AAAA,Inc.               9,126      9,126
210    Communications,Inc.     8,327                         8,327
219    Systems, Unlimited      6,852      6,852    6,852
222    ABEL Computers          4,675      4,675    4,675
224    Jones Electric         10,023     10,023
228    Suburban Sounds         4,882      4,882
232    Rainbow Drive,Inc.      3,707     (1,560)   5,267
241    Mercury Music Shop      3,988      3,988
243    Mason Stereo            9,497                                    9,497
246    Townsville Electronics 10,089     10,089
248    Vogue Computers         5,504                                    5,504
252    Celler Computers        8,528      8,528
256    Travis Tech Center      6,607      6,607
259    C & B Stereo            8,187               8,187
260    Audio Sounds            9,745      9,745
263    Audio Visual, Inc.      6,325      6,325
266    Electric Sound Center   1,926                         1,926
270    Ohio Ultrasound        13,421     13,421
274    Uptown Computers        4,849               4,849
276    Wonderful Music Co.     8,866      8,866
```

Assignment 3   61

					PAST DUE		
Acct. No.	Name	Balance	Current	Over 30	Over 60	Over 90	Comments
280	Transistor Electronics	6,968	6,968				
282	Biophonics, Ltd.	5,004	5,004				
284	Chuck's Computers	8,700	8,700				
289	Vista Sounds	3,226			3,226		
293	Victoria Electronics	9,940	9,940				
294	Sunny Sounds	6,469	6,469				
297	Panorama Stereo	9,794	9,794				
299	Pioneer Computers	7,263			7,263		
300	Atlas Computers	4,752	4,752				
301	Margarets'Stereo Center	4,919	4,919				
304	Pat's PC,Inc.	8,552	8,552				
307	Chicago Stereo,Inc.	1,700	1,700				
310	Carolyn's Computers	1,195	1,195				
312	Lawrence Electronics	5,558			5,558		
315	Dave's Radio & T.V.	5,425	5,425				
317	Hewer's Computer Center	7,934	7,934				
320	Suburbanville Computers	2,006		2,006			
321	Heisler Electronics	5,400	5,400				
324	Lundeen Stereo Center	10,060	10,060				
325	Downtown Techtronics	10,296	10,296				
326	General Computers	3,977		3,977			
327	Andre Sound Center	6,840		6,840			
329	Computerville	4,383	4,383				
330	Stereoville, Inc.	9,129	9,129				
334	BAUD Systems	14,744	9,594	5,150			
336	Microland	636	636				
337	Macroland	5,465	5,465				
339	Santa Sounds	3,173				3,173	
341	Michigan Systems	5,301		5,301			
342	Ohio Stereo	6,032	6,032				
343	Illinois Techtronics	9,380	9,380				
348	Indiana Stereo,Inc.	12,986	12,986				
352	Template Tech Center	5,066		5,066			
353	Zounds, Unlimited	9,027	9,027				
355	Quadraphonics	2,900	2,900				
356	Diskway Corp	7,673			7,673		
360	PC,Unlimited	7,439		7,439			
361	Comptech Corp	10,735	10,735				
365	Urban Electronics	8,944	8,944				
369	Allen Stereos	6,700	6,700				
370	Westland Sound Center	7,761	7,761				
372	Tapedeck Center	8,245		8,245			
375	Alma Computers	3,744	3,744				
378	McNab Computers	5,440	5,440				
383	Anderson Stereo Center	9,532	9,532				
386	Mets's Music Center	10,325	4,200	6,125			
388	Maas Electronics	8,835	6,760	2,075			

62 Assignment 3

392	Marv's Stereos	14,203	14,203		
395	Tony's Stereo	4,565			4,565
401	Donna's Stereo Center	6,152		6,152	
403	Scheerens Stereo	15,308	6,931	8,377	
406	Ed's Computer Center	8,030		3,163	4,867
	Totals	650,290	448,843	127,310	51,398	22,739

Audit Adjustments:

Balance per Audit

Assignment 3   63

COMMENTS FROM MANAGEMENT ON EQUIPMENT ACCOUNTS RECEIVABLE CONFIRMATIONS

All accounts and notes receivable were confirmed positively, while the smaller parts and supplies customers were sent negative confirmations. (See separate workpaper prepared by DHW.)

After scheduling replies, you meet with the Vice-Presidents of Finance and Marketing/Sales to discuss the differences and possible write-offs. The following notes reflect the result of your discussion regarding the specific exceptions:

Vista Sounds
Inspection of invoice indicates customer is correct. Client sent a revised statement showing a balance due in the amount of $3,186.

Biophonics, Ltd.
Good credit rating. No problems in the past.

Advanced Systems
Upon review of the documentation returned by the drivers, it appears that the customer is correct; the FM radio was not received.

Cato Processors
Customer is correct, even though merchandise was not yet received by Systems Direct. Systems Direct policy is to pay postage (freight) on returns. Credit customer account for $400.

Vogue Computers
A review of correspondence and collection efforts does not indicate any promise. Systems Direct agrees to a write-off.

Mason Stereo
Customer was sent a note but has not yet signed and returned it to Systems Direct. It has been several weeks. Correspondence and logs of telephone messages indicate some reluctance to sign the note. The client is opposed to a write-off but gives no evidence to support this position. You agree to delay a write-off.

Santa Sounds
Client agrees to a write-off.

Tony's Stereo
Customer continually promises to pay, but never does. Systems Direct is still optimistic. Tony's has been offered a note but has not yet signed it. You insist on writing off the account. Systems Direct balks but reluctantly agrees.

Ed's Computer Center
Confirmation indicated that customer would send partial payment soon. Client received $4,867 on January 10, 1991. You verified the receipt and the deposit ticket

McNab Computers
Customer is correct.

Alma Computers
Sent confirmation to wrong customer. Should be Albion Sounds. Check January cash receipts.

Accounts Receivable - Parts and Supplies
December 31, 1990

(This account was audited by your associate who made the following comments for the workpapers.)

Negative confirmations were sent to all parts and supplies customers with balances due as of December 31, 1990. The statements were mailed after comparing the statement balances with the printout furnished by the client and with the balance in the general ledger account and trial balance.

The statements were mailed first class in our firm's envelopes showing our firm's return address.

Summary of responses:

  8 statements were returned as undeliverable (i.e., addressee unknown, moved and left no forwarding address, etc.).
  12 replies were received indicating minor differences.

The above were reviewed with management. It was agreed that balances totalling $2,550 should be written off as uncollectible, and the accounts should be removed from the subsidiary ledger even though some additional collection efforts may be made.

Before being called to another audit, your associate made the following adjusting entry for you to add to those you make:

124	Allowance for Doubtful Accounts	2,550	
121	Accounts Receivable - Parts & Supplies		2,550
	To write off as uncollectible various account balances. List of accounts written off was given to the client.		

SYSTEMS DIRECT
123 State Street
Detroit, Michigan

January 2, 1991

Anderson Electronics
308 Champlain Ave.
Akron, Ohio

Please confirm the balance in your account in the amount of $8,519 of December 31, 1990, directly to our auditors:

        Smith and Weiss, CPAs
          Detroit, Michigan

A self-addressed, stamped envelope is enclosed for your convenience. A prompt reply to our auditors is appreciated.

This is not a request for payment.

J. Medina
J. Medina
Vice-President--Finance

The above balance is correct. _____

The above balance is incorrect as noted below. ✓

WE SENT IN A CHECK DECEMBER 29, 1990.

By: *J. Smith*
Date: 1/8/91

SYSTEMS DIRECT
123 State Street
Detroit, Michigan

January 2, 1991

Vista Sounds
606 Central Street
Toledo, Ohio

Please confirm the balance in your account in the amount of $ 3,226 of December 31, 1990, directly to our auditors:

        Smith and Weiss, CPAs
          Detroit, Michigan

A self-addressed, stamped envelope is enclosed for your convenience. A prompt reply to our auditors is appreciated.

This is not a request for payment.

J. Medina
J. Medina
Vice-President--Finance

The above balance is correct. _____

The above balance is incorrect as noted below.   X___

Correct balance is $3,186. Above includes $40 billing error. We have notified Systems Direct, but they have not adjusted our account. We'll pay when we receive a corrected statement.

By: *J. Clark*
Date: Jan. 7, 1991

Assignment 3   67

SYSTEMS DIRECT
123 State Street
Detroit, Michigan

January 2, 1991

Biophonics, Ltd.
20 Main Street
London, Ontario
CANADA

Please confirm the balance in your account in the amount of $5,004 of December 31, 1990, directly to our auditors:

Smith and Weiss, CPAs
Detroit, Michigan

A self-addressed, stamped envelope is enclosed for your convenience. A prompt reply to our auditors is appreciated.

This is not a request for payment.

J. Medina
J. Medina
Vice-President--Finance

The above balance is correct. _____

The above balance is incorrect as noted below. __X__

We pay by invoice, not by statement. Cannot confirm.

By: *J. White*
Date: *Jan. 9, 1991*

SYSTEMS DIRECT
123 State Street
Detroit, Michigan

January 2, 1991

Advanced Systems
14 Marquette Highway
South Bend, Indiana

Please confirm the balance in your account in the amount of $ 2,154 of December 31, 1990, directly to our auditors:

        Smith and Weiss, CPAs
           Detroit, Michigan

A self-addressed, stamped envelope is enclosed for your convenience. A prompt reply to our auditors is appreciated.

This is not a request for payment.

J. Medina
J. Medina
Vice-President--Finance

The above balance is correct. _____

The above balance is incorrect as noted below. _X_

Did not receive FM radios as ordered. The correct balance is $1,584.

By: *RJ Jones*
Date: *Jan 8, 1991*

SYSTEMS DIRECT
123 State Street
Detroit, Michigan

January 2, 1991

Cato Processors
1212 LaSalle Ave.
Cleveland, Ohio

Please confirm the balance in your account in the amount of $ 965 of December 31, 1990, directly to our auditors:

      Smith and Weiss, CPAs
        Detroit, Michigan

A self-addressed, stamped envelope is enclosed for your convenience. A prompt reply to our auditors is appreciated.

This is not a request for payment.

J. Medina
J. Medina
Vice-President--Finance

The above balance is correct. _____

The above balance is incorrect as noted below.   X

We ordered one word processor and you shipped two. One was returned. Our balance is $565.

By: *A. Brown*
Date: *1/10/91*

70   Assignment 3

SYSTEMS DIRECT
123 State Street
Detroit, Michigan

January 2, 1991

Vogue Computers
11 Arlington Street
South Bend, Indiana

Please confirm the balance in your account in the amount of $5,504 of December 31, 1990, directly to our auditors:

        Smith and Weiss, CPAs
          Detroit, Michigan

A self-addressed, stamped envelope is enclosed for your convenience. A prompt reply to our auditors is appreciated.

This is not a request for payment.

J. Medina
J. Medina
Vice-President--Finance

The above balance is correct. _____

The above balance is incorrect as noted below. _____

_____
_____
_____

By: _____
Date: _____

Returned by post office. Addressee unknown.

Assignment 3

SYSTEMS DIRECT
123 State Street
Detroit, Michigan

January 2, 1991

Mason Stereo
26 Broad Street
Flint, Michigan

Please confirm the balance in your account in the amount of $9,497 of December 31, 1990, directly to our auditors:

        Smith and Weiss, CPAs
          Detroit, Michigan

A self-addressed, stamped envelope is enclosed for your convenience. A prompt reply to our auditors is appreciated.

This is not a request for payment.

J. Medina
J. Medina
Vice-President--Finance

The above balance is correct. ✓

The above balance is incorrect as noted below. _____

We have signed a three-year note for this account.

By: *J. Zagers*
Date: *9 Jan 1991*

SYSTEMS DIRECT
123 State Street
Detroit, Michigan

January 2, 1991

Santa Sounds
4430 Main Street
Dayton, Ohio

Please confirm the balance in your account in the amount of $3,173 of December 31, 1990, directly to our auditors:

> Smith and Weiss, CPAs
> Detroit, Michigan

A self-addressed, stamped envelope is enclosed for your convenience. A prompt reply to our auditors is appreciated.

This is not a request for payment.

J. Medina
J. Medina
Vice-President--Finance

The above balance is correct. _____

The above balance is incorrect as noted below. _____

_____
_____
_____

By: _____
Date: _____

Returned by post office. Addressee moved, unable to forward.

Assignment 3

SYSTEMS DIRECT
123 State Street
Detroit, Michigan

January 2, 1991

Tony's Stereo
168 Hatch Street
Lansing, Michigan

Please confirm the balance in your account in the amount of $4,565 of December 31, 1990, directly to our auditors:

        Smith and Weiss, CPAs
          Detroit, Michigan

A self-addressed, stamped envelope is enclosed for your convenience. A prompt reply to our auditors is appreciated.

This is not a request for payment.

J. Medina
J. Medina
Vice-President--Finance

The above balance is correct.   *X*

The above balance is incorrect as noted below. _____

We will send something soon.

By: *Tony Miller*
Date: *Jan. 10, 1991*

SYSTEMS DIRECT
123 State Street
Detroit, Michigan

January 2, 1991

Ed's Computer Center
123 First Street
Fort Wayne, Indiana

Please confirm the balance in your account in the amount of $ 8,030 of December 31, 1990, directly to our auditors:

        Smith and Weiss, CPAs
          Detroit, Michigan

A self-addressed, stamped envelope is enclosed for your convenience. A prompt reply to our auditors is appreciated.

This is not a request for payment.

J. Medina
J. Medina
Vice-President--Finance

The above balance is correct.   __X__

The above balance is incorrect as noted below. _____

Will send something on account as soon as possible.
_____

By: _Ed Smith_
Date: _Jan. 8, 1991_

Assignment 3

SYSTEMS DIRECT
123 State Street
Detroit, Michigan

January 2, 1991

McNab Computers
216 Cross Road
Toledo, Ohio

Please confirm the balance in your account in the amount of $ 5,440 of December 31, 1990, directly to our auditors:

       Smith and Weiss, CPAs
         Detroit, Michigan

A self-addressed, stamped envelope is enclosed for your convenience. A prompt reply to our auditors is appreciated.

This is not a request for payment.

J. Medina
J. Medina
Vice-President--Finance

The above balance is correct. _____

The above balance is incorrect as noted below. _X_

Our records show a balance of $ 3,640.
_____

_____

By: *P. McNab*
Date: *Jan. 5, 1991*

SYSTEMS DIRECT
123 State Street
Detroit, Michigan

January 2, 1991

Albion Sounds
146 Decatur Drive
Bowling Green, Ohio

Please confirm the balance in your account in the amount of $ 4,411 of December 31, 1990, directly to our auditors:

        Smith and Weiss, CPAs
           Detroit, Michigan

A self-addressed, stamped envelope is enclosed for your convenience. A prompt reply to our auditors is appreciated.

This is not a request for payment.

J. Medina
J. Medina
Vice-President--Finance

The above balance is correct. _____

The above balance is incorrect as noted below. _____

We are Alma Computers. You sent this to the wrong address.
_____
_____

By: *Alan Alma*
Date: *Jan. 6, 1991*

Assignment 3

Systems Direct
Schedule of Notes Receivable (PBC)
December 31, 1990

File name: notesrec
Cells used: a1.g62

Maker	Date of Note	Original Amount of Note	Monthly Payment	Payments Made in 1990	Balance 12/31/90
A. & B Computers	12-1-90	12,000	333	0	12,000
Becky Stereo Center	3-1-90	7,200	200	1,200	6,000
B.& G. Electronics	6-1-90	25,200	700	4,200	21,000
Wisconsin Stereo, Inc.	2-1-90	25,920	720	7,200	18,720
Detroit Stereo Ctr.	6-1-90	16,200	450	2,700	13,500
Columbus Comp Land	8-1-90	28,080	780	3,120	24,960
Ann Arbor Electron.	2-1-90	21,600	600	6,000	15,600
Ypsilanti Stereoland	5-1-90	19,800	550	3,850	15,950
Toledo Sound Center	2-1-90	16,200	450	3,150	13,050
Totals		172,200		31,420	140,780

Audit notes:

This year the company began selling equipment to selected retailers by taking notes receivable over thirty-six monthly payments with the first payment due the month following the sale (date of note). Included in the faces of the notes is interest at 12 percent per annum.

For book purposes the company recognizes the sale on the accrual basis, but plans to report income for income tax purposes on the installment basis. The effective income tax rate for 1990 is 40%.

Gross profit on each sale is 25%, recognized for income tax purposes over the life of the note on a straight-line basis.

All notes have been positively confirmed except the Becky Stereo Center note, which was returned by the post office as undeliverable. Management agrees with your recommendation to write off this note even though management intends to pursue collection and/or repossession through its attorneys. Write off remaining balance after adjusting discount account for interest earned in 1990.

The following instructions are from your senior on the audit and are intended to assist you in completing the worksheet on the next page.

You are to do the following:

1. Verify the information on Lines A, B, and C with the information supplied above by the client.

2. Compute the present value of the notes and the original discount as required on Lines D and E. Payments made (Line F) is provided by the client and shown above. Line G shows the balance of the notes at December 31, before the writeoff of the Becky note. Interest earned during the year is calculated by deducting from the original discount (Line C), the discount at the end of the year (Line F).

3. Prepare the necessary adjusting entries.

Systems Direct
Notes Receivable - Worksheet
December 31, 1990

File name: notrecws
Cells used: a1.154

Line	Description	Totals	A & B Computers	Becky Stereo Center	B & G Electro.	Wisconsin Stereo	Detroit Stereo	Columbus Computer Land	Ann Arbor Electro.	Ypsilanti Stereo Land	Toledo Sound Center
A	Date of Note		12-1-90	3-1-90	6-1-90	2-1-90	6-1-90	8-1-90	2-1-90	5-1-90	2-1-90
B	Monthly payment		333	200	700	720	450	780	600	550	450
C	Original note amount	172,200	12,000	7,200	25,200	25,920	16,200	28,080	21,600	19,800	16,200
D	Original PV										
E (C-D)	Original discount										
F	Payments made - 1990										
G (C-F)	Balance 12/31/90										
H	AJE write off Becky note										
I (G-H)	Balance per audit		======	======	======	======	======	======	======	======	======

Discount on Notes Receivable (# 123)

	December 31, 1990:										
A	Original face value	172,200	12,000	7,200	25,200	25,920	16,200	28,080	21,600	19,800	16,200
B	Original present value										
C (A-B)	Original discount AJE ___										

Computation of discount:

D (G above)	Face value at 12-31-90	140,780	12,000	6,000	21,000	18,720	13,500	24,960	15,600	15,950	13,050
	Present value at 12/31/90:										
E	# of remaining payments Present value at 12/31/90		36	30	30	26	30	32	26	29	29
F (D-E)	Discount at 12/31/90										
G (C-F)	Reduction in discount (Interest earned in 1990) - AJE ___										
H	AJE Write off Becky note										
I (F-H)	Balance per audit		======	======	======	======	======	======	======	======	======
J (G above)	Interest earned - 1990		======	======	======	======	======	======	======	======	======

Assignment 3   79

Systems Direct
Unrealized Gross Profit on Notes Receivable
December 31, 1990

File name: unrealgp
Cells used: a1.l30

Line	Description	Totals	A & B Computers	Becky Stereo Center	B & G Electro.	Wisconsin Stereo	Detroit Stereo	Columbus Computer Land	Ann Arbor Electro.	Epsilanti Stereo Land	Toledo Sound Center
A	Original present value										
B(A*.25)	Total gross profit										
	Number of payments made in 1990										
	Percent of remaining payments at 12/31/90 (Ex. 30/36 = .8333)										
C	Unrealized gross profit at 12/31/90	======	======	======	======	======	======	======	======	======	======
D(B*C)	On income tax workpaper:	======									
	Reduce income tax payable by 40% of unrealized gross profit on notes receivable(40% * ------)										

80 Assignment 3

ALLOWANCE FOR DOUBTFUL ACCOUNTS (# 124)
DECEMBER 31, 1990

(Notes from management inquiries)

The client uses a monthly aging schedule to follow up on slow or nonpaying customers. As accounts approach 90 days without payment, the Vice-President—Finance contacts the customer and, if successful, arranges to convert the balance into a short-term note. If unsuccessful, the account is written off as uncollectible.

The allowance account receives charges from accounts receivable for equipment and for parts and supplies, as well as from uncollectible notes.

The bad debts expense account debit and the allowance account credit are estimated during the year for monthly statement purposes. They are computed at year-end by applying an experience ratio to the sales of equipment, software, parts, and supplies.

The experience ratio is a moving average computed by dividing gross sales of equipment, software, parts, and supplies into actual write-offs over a three-year period. The updated experience ratio is multiplied by the current year gross sales to determine the balance in the Bad Debts Expense account for the year.

You are to update the experience ratio by completing the schedule, compute the amount of the bad debts expense, and make the appropriate adjusting entry.

A copy of last year's workpaper and analysis follows.

The 1991 monthly recurring journal entry may be determined by taking one-twelfth of the final bad debts expense for 1990.

Assignment 3   81

```
Systems Direct                              File name:   allow
Allowance for Doubtful Accounts             Cells used:  a1.f114
Bad Debts Expense
Worksheet
December 31, 1990
                                              Allowance      Bad Debt
                                               Account       Expense
                                             -----------   -----------
Balance per Audit - 12/31/89                    43,480
Add: Eleven monthly recurring entries           99,000        99,000
                                              ---------     ---------
                                               142,480
Less: Actual write offs during 1990             90,460
                                              ---------     ---------
Balance per trial balance                       52,020        99,000
                                              ---------

Audit adjustments:
  (identify AJE's already made to
   write off uncollectible accounts)




                                              ---------


                                              ---------

Balance before adjustment to Bad Debt Exp.

AJE___ to adjust Bad Debt Expense per
experience ratio computation
                                              ---------     ---------
Balance per Audit - 12/31/90

                                              =========     =========

Audit adjustment:
```

82   Assignment 3

Systems Direct
Allowance for Doubtful Accounts (# 124)
Calculation of Experience Ratio

	Year	Gross Sales	Actual Write offs	Experience Rate
	1986	4,060,000	57,145	
	1987	4,750,000	69,940	
	1988	5,536,390	78,070	
	Totals	14,346,390	205,155	0.01430

1989 Experience Rate:
Add	1989	6,521,150	90,780	
Less	1986	(4,060,000)	(57,145)	
	Totals	16,807,540	238,790	0.01421

1990 Experience Rate:
  Add
  Less

        Totals

1989 computation of Bad Debt Expense:
    .0142 x 6,521,150 = 92,600

1990 computation of Bad Debt Expense:

    Balance per trial balance   99,000

    Adjustment

1990 Gross Sales: (before adjustments)
 # 600 Equipment
 # 601 Parts and Supplies

         Totals
Audit Adjustments

Balance for computing experience ratio

Actual 1990 writeoffs
    From analysis of allowance account above   90,460
Audit adjustments:

Total actual writeoffs - 1990

Assignment 3   83

ASSIGNMENT 4

INVENTORY, PAYABLES, COST OF SALES

AUDIT PROGRAM

Summary of assignment:

Test purchase cutoff.

Complete inventory count sheets.

Test for purchase discounts.

Perform pricing tests.

Test for obsolete inventory.

Review January check register for unrecorded payables.

Allocate freight-in between inventory and cost of sales. (This will not be completed until a subsequent assignment.)

General

		Initial	Date

1. Foot and crossfoot lead schedule and all other PBC schedules, if any. ____ ____

2. Compare balances on other PBC schedules, if any, with balances on lead schedule. ____ ____

3. Compare balances on lead schedule with account balances in the trial balance. ____ ____

Analytical Review Procedures

1. Note any unusual relationships between current and prior years' accounts, including the following: purchases, returns and allowances, discounts, inventories, and payables. *DHW* ____

2. Scan for unusual entries to above accounts (i.e., debits to accounts payable from other than check register, etc.). *DHW* ____

3. Analyze all general journal entries to these accounts. *DHW* ____

Other Substantive Audit Procedures

Inventories   Initial   Date

1. Review client's inventory taking instructions. ____ ____

2. Make test counts of selected inventory items. *DHW* ____

3. Trace physical test counts to client's final inventory printout. *DHW* ____

4. Using client's final inventory listing:

   a. Verify arithmetic accuracy. *DHW* ____

   b. Test unit prices to recent vendor's invoices. ____ ____

   c. Agree total per PBC schedule to trial balance. ____ ____

5. Test for obsolete inventory. Suggest write-off of any inventory with no sales within the previous 12 months. ____ ____

6. Perform purchase cutoff tests for potential inventory in transit. *DHW* ____

7. Determine whether any inventory is located off premises (i.e., consigned out). *DHW* ____

8. Check for pledged inventory and/or purchase commitments. *DHW* ____

9. Allocate freight-in on purchases between inventory and cost of sales. ____ ____

10. Determine proper financial statement classification and disclosure. ____ ____

Accounts Payable (Trade)

1. Determine if appropriate to request positive confirmations from selected vendors. *DHW* ____

2. On a test basis:

   a. Examine completeness of vouchers, noting purchase orders, receiving reports, invoices, and copies of checks. Check for proper destruction to prohibit resubmission for duplicate payment. *DHW* ___

b. Trace payment to check register. *DHW* ___

c. Note whether client takes discount. *DHW* ___

d. Note proper approvals. *DHW* ___

3. Examine purchase cutoff procedures to determine that purchases (as well as inventories and payables) are recorded in the proper period. ___ ___

a. Review vendors' invoices in the purchase journal, or voucher register, for several days before and after year-end, and compare with receiving reports. *DHW* ___

b. Review purchase returns after year-end for proper authorization and recording, and compare with supporting documentation (shipping records, memoranda, etc.). *DHW* ___

4. Review check register for transactions recorded after the balance sheet date. ___ ___

5. Review cash disbursements (check register) after the balance sheet date for unrecorded liabilities. ___ ___

Comment from senior accountant:
December purchases are all in inventory; hence, discounts on these invoices are to be credited to inventory.

Required:

1. Complete the audit program.
2. Complete the lead schedule.
3. Turn in the following in the order listed:

   a. Time budget

   b. Audit program

   c. Lead schedule

   d. Adjusting journal entries with complete explanations

   e. Inventory—Equipment and Software

   f. Inventory—Parts and Supplies

   g. Freight-in allocation worksheet

   h. Accounts Payable—Trade

Systems Direct
Inventory Lead Schedule (PBC)
Cost of Sales
Freight-In on Purchases
Accounts Payable - Trade
December 31, 1990

File name: invlead
Cells used: a1.h37

Acct. No.	Account Title	Per T/B	#	Adjustments Debit	#	Credit	Per Audit
Inventories:							
130	Equipment and soft.	575,525					
131	Parts and supplies	15,373					
	Totals	590,898					
Cost of sales:							
700	Equipment and soft.	4,307,531					
701	Parts and supplies	978,111					
	Totals	5,285,642					
Freight-in on purchases:							
710	Freight-in	155,800					
	Totals	155,800					
300	Accounts Payable - Trade	487,519					

Audit adjustments:

86 Assignment 4

Systems Direct
Inventory - Equip. & Software
Summary of Count Sheets
(Prepared by DHW)
December 31, 1990

File name: inveneqp
Cells used: a1.d47

Electronic Sound Systems:	Qty.	Unit Cost	Total Cost
Self-contained stereos	300	425	
Turntables	300	110	
Speakers	300	140	
Amplifier/Receivers	300	160	
AM/FM Radios	300	120	
Total			
Computers:			
H-H - 256's	40	400	
Pear - 320's	50	550	
Analog - 512's	56	750	
Digitel - 320's	64	600	
Wong - 512's	36	650	
IMA - 320's	60	550	
Admiral 64's	100	220	
NAC Printers	50	170	
Mobile 512 portables	50	350	
Total			
Software:			
Cambridge Word Processors	100	150	
San Jose Spreadsheet	83	175	
IMA Data base Management	100	180	
Games packages	110	120	
Total			
Total Inventory			

Audit adjustments:

    Balance per audit

Assignment 4   87

SMITH & WEISS
Certified Public Accountants

93 Third Street
Detroit, Michigan

```
          Inventory - Equipment
              Audit Memo
           December 31, 1990
```

I made test counts of client's computer equipment, software, and electronic sound systems on hand at January 2, 1991, traced these counts to the client's lists, and prepared the attached summary count sheets.

I tested several prices to vendors' invoices, but year-end payables and vendors' invoices were not yet available.

The client maintains the inventories on a first-in, first-out (FIFO) basis, so it is important to check some year-end vendors' invoices for prices to be used in year-end inventories.

There has been no sale of Admiral 64 computers during the last twelve months and these units are virtually unsalable. Management has agreed to write these off as a loss this year, but has no plans at this time as to disposition of these units. Any proceeds from ultimate sale would be minimal and not material and could be recorded as other income in the year of sale.

                                        D.H.W. 1/3/91

Systems Direct
Inventory - Parts and Supplies
Summary of Count Sheets
(Prepared by DHW)
December 31, 1990

File name: invenp&s
Cells used: a1.e39

	Total FIFO Cost	
Sound Equipment-Parts and Supplies:		
Speakers	2,125	
Tapes and Cassettes	1,950	
Tools	375	
Support Hardware:		
Wires	350	
Connections	175	
Other	575	5,550
Computer Parts and Supplies:		
Diskettes (Boxes of 10)	2,325	
Paper	950	
Ribbons	3,075	
Support Hardware:		
Wire	225	
Connections	150	
Other	600	7,325
Total Inventory - Parts and Supplies		12,875

Audit adjustments:
  See attached memo on substantive audit procedures.

Balance per trial balance
Balance per audit   12,875

AJE ___

SMITH & WEISS
Certified Public Accountants

93 Third Street
Detroit, Michigan

Inventory - Parts and Supplies
Audit Memo
December 31, 1990

I made test counts of parts and supplies on hand at January 2, 1991, and traced these counts to the client's lists. I also tested several prices to vendors' invoices and found no errors.

Cutoff tests were made to determine that there is no inventory in transit at year-end.

The client uses an average markup to cost its parts and supplies sales during the year. Consequently, the actual physical inventory determined by year-end physical count may not agree with the ledger account balance. In prior years, the adjusting entry made at year-end resulted in a write-down from the ledger to the actual inventory.

DHW 1/2/91

Interoffice Memorandum

To: All employees participating in taking inventory
From: Rosanna Hanna, Chief Accountant
Date: December 21, 1990

Subject: Procedures for taking inventory on Friday and Saturday, December 30 and 31, 1990

Report to the warehouse on Friday at 3:00 PM and Saturday at 9:00 AM. You are expected to work until at least 3:00 PM on Saturday. Lunch will be provided.

The physical inventory will be taken Saturday in teams of two. One person will count the items while the second person records the count called out by the first person.

A second count will be made after lunch with the teams reversed (the counter will now be the recorder).

Instructions for Friday:
Each inventory item (group) will have attached or associated with it two IMA computer cards. Each card has preprinted on it the product description, number, and location.

> Card 1. Blue stripe across the top.
> Card 2. Green stripe across the top.

The Friday crew will see that these cards are available and properly associated with the inventory group. They will also become familiar with the location and layout of the inventory.

Instructions for Saturday:
As you report, you will be assigned a partner and told which area of the warehouse you will cover.

Your team will proceed to count and record quantities of each inventory item on Card 1 (blue stripe), using the porta-punch to punch quantity counts on the card with the stylus (pointed instrument).

After you have completed your initial count, you are to turn in your blue-striped cards to the computer room for processing.

After lunch, you will repeat the count procedure reversing the team roles (the counter is now the recorder), recording the quantities on the green-striped cards.

Upon completion, you are to turn in the green-striped cards and the white cards to the computer room. This completes your assignment.

Instructions to computer room personnel:
As each group of cards is received, sort by product number.

When both groups of cards have been received and sorted, process them through the collator. Those cards whose counts agree will be accumulated in one stack. Cards with differences in counts will be kicked aside in a separate stack. This stack of cards will be run through the printer to obtain a printout of exceptions between each count.

The items on the exception printout will be recounted by a separate team. Another printout will be run following the recount. This procedure should result in as accurate an inventory count as possible.

Your usual cooperation in this effort is appreciated.

Systems Direct
Freight-In Allocation Worksheet
December 31, 1990

File name: freight
Cells used: a1.g58

Audit note:
The client charges all freight on equipment purchases to a freight-in account (Acct. # 710). Freight on parts and supplies is negligible. Accordingly, at year-end, you are to allocate the freight-in balance after all audit adjustments have been posted between inventory and cost of sales. The allocation is to be based on the proportion of the equipment inventory to equipment cost of sales. Your senior has prepared the following worksheet to assist you and reminds you that you will not be able to complete this schedule until you have reviewed other accounts payable for any unpaid freight invoices.

Freight-in:
  Balance per trial balance   155,800
  Audit adjustments:

                                              -------   -------
  Balance before allocation *
                                                          =======

Inventory - Equipment:
  Balance per trial balance   575,525
  Audit adjustments:

                                              -------   -------
Balance before allocation **
                                                       =======

Cost of sales - Equipment:
  Balance per trial balance   4,307,531
  Audit adjustment(s):

Balance before allocation #
                                                   =========

    Inventory - Equipment **
    Cost of Sales - Eqpt. #

    Inventory and Cost of
    Sales(denominator)***
                        =========

Allocation formula:

    Inventory - Equipment**
    -----------------------   x   Freight before allocation =
    Inventory and Cost of   =========
    Sales(denominator)***

Audit adjustment:

Assignment 4   93

```
Systems Direct                              File name:   acctpay
Accounts Payable - Trade (PBC)              Cells used:  a1.h44
December 31, 1990
```

Vendor	Gross	Disc.	Net	Check #
Cambridge Word Processors	12,240	240	12,000	91116
Pear Computer Company	23,100	440	22,660	91115
Wong Computers, Inc.	33,700	650	33,050	91118
Speakers, Ltd.	22,200	420	21,780	91122
IMA Corp.	32,400	622	31,778	91117
Panorama Electronics, Ltd.	73,150	1,330	71,820	91124
Turntables, Ltd.	23,500	440	23,060	91107
Analog Computer Corp.	40,800	750	40,050	91119
Hewlett Hudson	20,900	400	20,500	91120
RSC, Inc.	30,030	572	29,458	91125
Xenio Corp.	17,800	350	17,450	91105
Digitel, Inc.	32,100	600	31,500	91126
San Jose Software, Inc.	17,650	350	17,300	91127
Games, Inc.	12,150	240	11,910	91128
Unicorn Mfg. Co.	24,300	425	23,875	91129
Various parts & supply vendors	71,499 *E*	0	71,499	various *T*
Total Trade Payables	487,519	7,829	479,690	

Audit adjustments:

    Sub-totals

    Balance per audit

Tickmarks:
    CF = Crossfooted schedule
    E = Examined underlying documentation - vendors' invoices
        supporting documentation
    F = Footed schedule
    T/B = Agrees with trial balance
    T = Traced to entry in January check register
    V = Calculation verified

INVOICE

CAMBRIDGE WORD PROCESSORS, INC.
100 Third Street
Cambridge, Massachusetts

DATE: December 10, 1990

SOLD TO: Systems Direct
123 State Street
Detroit, Michigan

DELIVER TO: Same

Terms: 2/30/N45 F.O.B. SHIPPING POINT

QUANTITY	DESCRIPTION	UNIT COST	TOTAL COST
80	Cambridge Word Processors	$150	$12,000

RECEIVED V.V. 12/14/90 — Thank You

FREIGHT 240
TOTAL – BALANCE DUE $12,240

PEAR COMPUTER COMPANY, INC.
1425 Industrial Blvd., La Jolla, California

INVOICE

DATE: 12/5/89

SOLD TO: Systems Direct
123 State Street
Detroit, Michigan

SHIP TO: Same

Terms: 1/10, n/30, FOB Detroit

QUANTITY	DESCRIPTION	UNIT COST	TOTAL COST
40	Pear – System 320	$550	$22,000

RECEIVED V.V. 12/7/90

FREIGHT 1,100
TOTAL – BALANCE DUE $23,100

Thank You

INVOICE
WONG COMPUTERS, INC.
4 Salem Street
Methuen, Massachusetts

DATE: Dec. 14, 1990

SOLD TO: Systems Direct
123 State Street
Detroit, Michigan

DELIVER TO: Same

Terms: 2/30/N45   F.O.B. SHIPPING POINT

QUANTITY	DESCRIPTION	UNIT COST	TOTAL COST
50	Wong-System 512	$650	$32,500

RECEIVED
E.M.
12/19/90

Thank You

FREIGHT 1,200
TOTAL – BALANCE DUE $33,700

SPEAKERS, LTD.
Longharn Road
Waco, Texas

INVOICE

SOLD TO: Systems Direct
123 State Street
Detroit, Michigan

SHIP TO: Same

DATE: 12/2/90

Terms: 1/10, n/30, FOB Detroit

QUANTITY	DESCRIPTION	UNIT COST	TOTAL COST
150	Speakers	$140	$21,000

RECEIVED
V.V.
12/7/90

Thank You

FREIGHT 1,200
TOTAL – Balance Due 22,200

INVOICE

IMA CORPORATION
220 Fourth Street
Albany, New York

DATE: Dec. 6, 1990

SOLD TO: Systems Direct
123 State Street
Detroit, Michigan

DELIVER TO: Same

Terms: 2/30/N45   F.O.B. SHIPPING POINT

QUANTITY	DESCRIPTION	UNIT COST	TOTAL COST
50	IMA-System 320	$550	$27,500
20	IMA Data Base Program	180	3,600

RECEIVED E.M. 12/11/90

FREIGHT: 1,300
TOTAL – BALANCE DUE: $32,400

Thank You

PANORAMA ELECTRONICS, LTD.
2-2-1, Sarugaku-cho
Tokyo, Japan

INVOICE

DATE: 7 Dec 1990

SOLD TO: Systems Direct
123 State Street
Detroit, Michigan

SHIP TO: Same

Terms: 1/10, n/30, FOB Detroit

QUANTITY	DESCRIPTION	UNIT COST	TOTAL COST
100	Self-Contained Stereos	$425	$42,500
200	AM/FM Radios	120	24,000

RECEIVED E.M. 12/11/90

FREIGHT: 6,650
TOTAL – BALANCE DUE: $73,150

Thank You

Assignment 4

INVOICE

TURNTABLES, LTD.
Champstead Road
London, England

DATE: Dec. 12, 1990

SOLD TO: Systems Direct
123 State Street
Detroit, Michigan

DELIVER TO: Same

Terms: 2/30/N45   F.O.B. SHIPPING POINT

QUANTITY	DESCRIPTION	UNIT COST	TOTAL COST
200	Turntables	$110	$22,000
		FREIGHT	1,500
		TOTAL – BALANCE DUE	$23,500

RECEIVED V.V. 12/19/90

Thank You

ANALOG COMPUTERS CORP.
2020 Massachusetts Avenue
Cambridge, Massachusetts

INVOICE

SOLD TO: Systems Direct
123 State Street
Detroit, Michigan

SHIP TO: Same

DATE: Dec. 12, 1990

Terms: 1/10, n/30, FOB Detroit

QUANTITY	DESCRIPTION	UNIT COST	TOTAL COST
50	Analog-System 512	$750	$37,500
		FREIGHT	3,300
		TOTAL – BALANCE DUE	$40,800

RECEIVED V.V. 12/17/90

Thank You

INVOICE

HEWLETT–HUDSON CORPORATION
23 Rialto Drive
Houston, Texas

DATE: Dec. 3, 1990

SOLD TO: Systems Direct
123 State Street
Detroit, Michigan

DELIVER TO: Same

Terms: 2/30/N45   F.O.B. SHIPPING POINT

QUANTITY	DESCRIPTION	UNIT COST	TOTAL COST
50	HH-System 256	$400	$20,000

RECEIVED E.M. 12/5/90

FREIGHT: 900
TOTAL – BALANCE DUE: $20,900

Thank You

RSC, Inc.
56 Prince Andrew Place
Don Mills, Canada

INVOICE

SOLD TO: Systems Direct
123 State Street
Detroit, Michigan

SHIP TO: Same

DATE: Dec. 5, 1990

Terms: 1/10, n/30, FOB Detroit

QUANTITY	DESCRIPTION	UNIT COST	TOTAL COST
160	Amplifier/Receiver	$160	$25,600
25	AM/FM Radios	120	3,000

RECEIVED E.M. 12/10/90

FREIGHT: 1,430
TOTAL – BALANCE DUE: $30,030

Thank You

Assignment 4

INVOICE

XENIO CORPORATION
2 Bay Drive
Ann Harbor, Michigan

DATE: Dec. 7, 1990

SOLD TO: Systems Direct
123 State Street
Detroit, Michigan

DELIVER TO: Same

Terms: 2/30/N45   F.O.B. SHIPPING POINT

QUANTITY	DESCRIPTION	UNIT COST	TOTAL COST
50	Mobile Lap Top Computers	$350	$17,500

RECEIVED V.V. 12/11/90

FREIGHT: 300
TOTAL – BALANCE DUE: $17,800

Thank You

DIGITEL, INC.
96 Trapelo Road
Waltham, Massachusetts

INVOICE

SOLD TO: Systems Direct
123 State Street
Detroit, Michigan

SHIP TO: Same

DATE: Dec. 10, 1990

Terms: 2/30/N45   F.O.B. SHIPPING POINT

QUANTITY	DESCRIPTION	UNIT COST	TOTAL COST
50	DIGITEL SYSTEM 320	$600	$30,000

RECEIVED B.K. 12/10/90

FREIGHT: 2,100
TOTAL – BALANCE DUE: $32,100

Thank You

Assignment 4

INVOICE

SAN JOSE SOFTWARE, INC.
1172 Ocean Blvd.
San Jose, California

DATE: Dec. 8, 1990

SOLD TO: Systems Direct
123 State Street
Detroit, Michigan

DELIVER TO: Same

Terms: 2/30/N45   F.O.B. SHIPPING POINT

QUANTITY	DESCRIPTION	UNIT COST	TOTAL COST
100	San Jose Spreadsheet	$175	$17,500

RECEIVED V.V. 12/11/90

FREIGHT: 150
TOTAL – BALANCE DUE: $17,650

Thank You

GAMES, INC.
72 Third Street
Oakland, California

INVOICE

SOLD TO: Systems Direct
123 State Street
Detroit, Michigan

SHIP TO: Same

DATE: Dec. 12, 1990

Terms: 2/30/N45   F.O.B. SHIPPING POINT

QUANTITY	DESCRIPTION	UNIT COST	TOTAL COST
100	Games – Software	$120	$12,000

RECEIVED E.M. 12/14/90

FREIGHT: 150
TOTAL – BALANCE DUE: $12,150

Thank You

INVOICE

Unicorn Manufacturing Co.
3–1 Song Tae
Taipei, Taiwan

DATE: Dec. 15, 1990

SOLD TO: Systems Direct
123 State Street
Detroit, Michigan

DELIVER TO: Same

Terms: 2/30/N45   F.O.B. SHIPPING POINT

QUANTITY	DESCRIPTION	UNIT COST	TOTAL COST
50	Self-Contained Stereos	$425	$21,250

RECEIVED V.V. 12/21/90

Thank You

FREIGHT: 3,050
TOTAL – BALANCE DUE: $24,300

Mobile Computer Mfg. Corp.
72 Industrial Drive
El Paso, Texas

INVOICE

SOLD TO: Systems Direct
123 State Street
Detroit, Michigan

SHIP TO: Same

DATE: Dec. 27, 1990

Terms: 2/30/N45   F.O.B. SHIPPING POINT

QUANTITY	DESCRIPTION	UNIT COST	TOTAL COST
50	Mobile Laptop Computers	$350	$17,500

RECEIVED V.V. 12/31/90

Thank You

FREIGHT: 1,720
TOTAL – BALANCE DUE: $19,220

INVOICE

NAC PRINTER MFG. CORP.
3–6–1, Kushogo–cho
Tokyo, Japan

DATE: Dec. 15, 1990

SOLD TO: Systems Direct
123 State Street
Detroit, Michigan

DELIVER TO: Same

Terms: 2/30/N45   F.O.B. SHIPPING POINT

QUANTITY	DESCRIPTION	UNIT COST	TOTAL COST
50	NAC Printers	$170	$8500

RECEIVED
E.M.
12/24/90

Thank You

FREIGHT: 850
TOTAL – BALANCE DUE: $9,350

Assignment 4   103

ASSIGNMENT 5

OTHER CURRENT ASSETS

(Prepaid Expenses)

AUDIT PROGRAM

Summary of assignment:

Client records monthly journal entries estimating these expenses for monthly income statements.

Prepare entry to adjust both the prepaid and related expense accounts after determining the balance per audit.

General

                                        Initial   Date

1. Foot and crossfoot lead schedule and all other PBC schedules (i.e., analysis of account 140, and prepaid insurance schedule).

2. Compare balances on lead schedule with account balances in the trial balance.

3. Compare balances on other PBC schedules with balances on lead schedule.

Analytical Review Procedures

1. Review entries in these accounts for the period and investigate large or unusual items.

Other Substantive Audit Procedures

1. Agree balances per lead schedules to general ledger account(s).   *DHW*

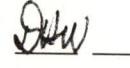

2. Examine policies, noting insurer, description and amount of insurance coverage, period covered, and premium.   *DHW*

3. Examine other supporting documentation.   *DHW*

                                        Initial   Date

4. Trace payments charged to prepaid expense to cash disbursements journal or check register.   *DHW*

5. Compare coverage confirmed by agent to coverage listed on schedule.

6. Compare amount of insurance coverage on building and equipment with estimated replacement costs to verify that adequate insurance is maintained.   *DHW*

7. Recompute prepaid expenses at balance sheet date and the related expenses for the year. Prepare adjusting entry(ies), if needed.

8. Review for proper financial statement classification and disclosure.

9. Compute expense amounts for 1991 monthly recurring journal entries.

Required:

1. Complete the audit program.
2. Complete the lead schedule.
3. Turn in the following in the order listed:

   a. Time budget

   b. Audit program

   c. Completed prepaid expense lead schedule

   d. Adjusting entries with complete explanations

   e. Analysis of prepaid expenses

   f. Prepaid insurance schedule

```
Systems Direct                           File name:    preplead
Prepaid Expenses Lead Schedule (PBC)     Cells used:   a1.h44
Insurance Expense
Professional Services Expense
Taxes and Licenses Expense
December 31, 1990


  Acct.                           Per          Adjustments            Per
   No.    Account Title           T/B    #   Debit    #   Credit     Audit
  -----   ---------------------  -------   --------  --  --------  ---------

   140    Prepaid Expenses        45,750

   815    Insurance Expense       22,000

   819    Professional Services   28,600


   821    Taxes and Licenses      66,000



Audit adjustments:
```

Assignment 5

Systems Direct
Prepaid Expenses Analyses (PBC)
December 31, 1990

File name: prepexp
Cells used: a1.j95

	Date	Insurance	Profess. Services	Taxes & Licenses	Prepaid Expenses # 140
Beginning balances		8,400			8,400 T
Debits (from check register):					
Acme Ins.-Workmen's comp.	1/31/90	1,500 E			1,500
Acme Ins. -Fidelity bonds	4/30	4,000 E			4,000
Acme Ins.-Fire-Bldg/Contents	7/31	10,200 E			10,200
Acme Ins.- Personal Liability	9/30	15,000 E			15,000
Dr. D.French - Flu shots-empl.	2/28		1,000 E		1,000
Brown & Beaver, Attys. 1/4 ret.	3/31		2,500 E		2,500
Jones & Son CPA's audit fee	4/30		19,500 E		19,500
Jones & Son CPA's tax return	5/31		5,000 E		5,000
Brown & Beaver, Attys. 2/4 ret.	6/30		2,500 E		2,500
Brown & Beaver, Attys. 3/4 ret.	9/30		2,500 E		2,500
Brown & Beaver, Attys. - lease	10/31		3,000 E		3,000
City of Detroit - 1/2 '90 R.E.Tax	1/2/90			6,125 E	6,125
City of Detroit '90 Bus. Lic. (1)	1/31			22,500 E	22,500
Treas. of MI '90 Reg./Franch. fee	1/31			500 E	500
City of Detroit-1989 adjustment	3/28			2,325 E	2,325
City of Detroit '90 Prop. taxes	4/30			4,500 E	4,500
Treas. of MI '90 vehicle lic.	4/30			2,675 E	2,675
City of Detroit - 2/2 '90 R.E.Tax	6/30			6,125 E	6,125
City of Detroit '90 Bus. License	7/31			30,000 E	30,000
(see note on business license)					
City of Detroit - 1/2 '91 R.E.Tax	12/31/90			12,500 E	12,500
Total debits incl. beg. bal.		39,100	36,000	87,250	162,350 T
Credits (from recurring monthly journal):					
	1/31/90	2,000	2,600	6,000	
	2/28	2,000	2,600	6,000	
	3/31	2,000	2,600	6,000	
	4/30	2,000	2,600	6,000	
	5/31	2,000	2,600	6,000	
	6/30	2,000	2,600	6,000	
	7/31	2,000	2,600	6,000	
	8/31	2,000	2,600	6,000	
	9/30	2,000	2,600	6,000	
	10/31	2,000	2,600	6,000	
	11/30	2,000	2,600	6,000	
Total credits		22,000	28,600	66,000	116,600 T
Balance per trial balance		17,100	7,400	21,250	45,750
Audit adjustment:					
Balance per audit		========	========	========	========

Assignment 5

Note:
> The business license is paid for each calendar year in semiannual installments in January and July, and is based on estimated sales for the next six months. In March of the following year an adjustment is made based on the actual sales of the previous year. In settlement, either a check is sent for the balance due, or a credit is taken and applied to the following year.

1989 Computation:

Sales - Equipment & Software	4,891,900
Sales - Parts and Supplies	1,629,250
Total sales subject to license	6,521,150
Total actual license (x .0075)	48,909
Paid during year (1989)	46,584
Additional 1989 liability	2,325

1990 Computation:

Audit adjustment:

Assignment 5

Systems Direct
Prepaid Insurance Schedule (PBC)
December 31, 1990

File name: insuranc
Cells used: a1.j28

| | Period Covered | | Prepaid | Paid | Expense | Prepaid |
Type	From	To	12/31/89	1990	1990	12/31/90
Fire - Building and Contents	7/1/89	6/30/90 E	2,150			
#88RI-211652	7/1/90	6/30/91 E		10,200		
Personal Liability	9/1/89	8/31/90 E	4,000			
#88RI880199	9/1/90	8/31/91 E		15,000		
Workmen's Comp	1/1/89	12/31/89 E				
#8211549	1/1/90	12/31/90 E		1,500		
Fidelity Bond	4/1/89	3/31/90 E	2,250			
#EF4448250	4/1/90	3/31/91 E		4,000		
Totals			8,400	30,700	0	0

E = Examined underlying document (insurance policy)
T = Traced to confirmation
F = Footed schedule
CF = Crossfooted totals
V = Vouched payment to check register

(Letter from Acme Insurance Agency)

ACME INSURANCE AGENCY, INC.

726 Lakeside Blvd.
Detroit, Michigan

Smith and Weiss, CPA's   January 12, 1991
Detroit, Michigan

Gentlemen:

Per your request, we are pleased to confirm the following insurance coverage of Systems Direct, as of December 31, 1990.

1. Empire Insurance Company:
    Workmen's Compensation Policy #8211549
    Coverage: $250,000 per occurrence
    Policy expires: December 31, 1990.
    Premium paid: $1,500

2. Employees' Fidelity, Inc.:
    Fidelity Bond #EF 4448250
    Coverage: $10,000 per employee on and off premises
    Policy expires: March 31, 1991
    Premium paid: $4,000

3. Ramadan Insurance Company:
    Fire Policy #88 RI 880199
    Coverage: Building - $1,500,000; Contents - $500,000
    Policy expires: June 30, 1991
    Premium paid: $10,200

4. Ramadan Insurance Company:
    Personal Injury Liability Policy #88 RI 211652
    Coverage: Limit $1,000,000 per person per accident
    Policy expires: August 31, 1991
            Premium paid: $15,000

Premiums paid during 1990 total $30,700.
Balance due at December 31, 1990 - $ 0.

We hope this information is helpful. Should you have any questions, please call us.

Sincerely,

R.M. Hansen, President

PLANT, PROPERTY, AND EQUIPMENT

AUDIT PROGRAM

Summary of assignment:

Prepare adjusting entry to correct posting to the repairs and maintenance accounts.

Correct recording of disposal of asset.

Adjust depreciation expense.

Capitalize a lease, the lease obligation, and record the interest for the year.

General

                                              Initial Date

1. Foot and crossfoot lead schedule and all other PBC schedules (i.e., fixed asset and depreciation) ____ ____

2. Compare balances on other PBC schedules with balances on lead schedule. ____ ____

3. Compare balances on lead schedules with account balances in the trial balance. ____ ____

4. Understand client posting regarding:

    a. Minimum amount to capitalize *DHW* ____

    b. Depreciation in year of acquisition and disposition *DHW* ____

    c. Estimated lives, terminal value, and methods of depreciation *DHW* ____

5. Review minutes for proper authorization to enter into lease agreement, and verify proper accounting. (May be left until Assignment 8.) ____ ____

Analytical Review and Substantive Procedures

1. Review general ledger accounts, noting any unusual entries. *DHW* ____

2. Review minutes for authorization for acquisitions and disposals, if appropriate. *DHW* ____

Other Substantive Procedures

                                              Initial Date

1. Analyze the following general ledger accounts:

    a. Repairs and Maintenance Expense ____ ____

    b. Depreciation expense accounts ____ ____

    c. Gain/Loss—Disposal of Fixed Assets ____ ____

2. Review computation of depreciation expense for the year. ____ ____

3. Compare acquisitions and dispositions with underlying documentation, noting differences, if any. Trace such transactions to cash disbursements and cash receipts. *DHW* ____

4. Review supporting documentation of entries to the repairs and maintenance expense account. *DHW* ____

5. Review insurance coverage in comparison to replacement or current plant, property, and equipment values. *DHW* ____

6. Prepare appropriate footnote to the financial statements on accounting policies. ____ ____

7. Compute depreciation and lease amortization for 1991 recurring general journal. (may be left until Assignment 8) ____ ____

Required:

1. Complete audit program.
2. Complete lead schedule.
3. Turn in the following in the order listed:

    a. Time budget

    b. Audit program

    c. Plant, Property, and Equipment—Lead Schedule

d. Adjusting entries with explanations

e. Property, plant, and equipment depreciation schedule, with calculations verified and audit adjustments, if any, reflected, and next year's depreciation expense calculated for next year's recurring monthly general journal entries

f. Completed repairs and maintenance schedule

g. Completed fixed asset additions and dispositions schedule

h. Lease calculation schedule (may be left until Assignment 8)

```
Systems Direct                                    File name:  ppelead
Plant, Property, Equipment Lead Schedule (PBC)    Cells used: a1.h54
December 31, 1990

Acct.                          Per            Adjustments              Per
No.    Account Title           T/B     #   Debit    #   Credit        Audit
-----  ---------------------   -----   --  -------  --  -------       -------
 200   Land                     50,000

 210   Building              1,250,000

 220   Trucks and Cars         173,000

 230   Warehouse Equipment      20,000

 240   Office Equipment         67,000

 250   Leasehold                18,000
                             ----------  ---------    -------       ---------
       Totals                1,578,000          0          0               0
                             ==========  =========    =======       =========

Accumulated Depreciation:
 211   Building                122,913

 221   Trucks and Cars         110,525

 231   Warehouse Equipment      12,288

 241   Office Equipment         50,825

 251   Leasehold                     0
                             ----------  ---------    -------       ---------
       Totals                  296,551          0          0               0
                             ==========  =========    =======       =========
```

(over)

Assignment 6   111

Depreciation Expense:
- 810 Building   22,913
- 811 Trucks and cars   26,400
- 812 Warehouse Equipment 2,288
- 813 Office Eqpt.   11,825
- 814 Leasehold   0

Totals	63,426	0	0	0

820 Repairs and Maint.   18,750

Audit adjustments:

```
Systems Direct                          File name:   deprsch
Plant, Property and Equipment           Cells used:  a1.j73
Depreciation Schedule
December 31, 1990

   Building # 210                S.L. 50 years - No salvage
   Trucks and Cars # 220         DDB 4 years
   Warehouse Equipment # 230     S.L. 8 years - No salvage
   Office Equipment # 240        S.L. 5 years - No salvage
   Lease # 250                   S.L. 20 years - No salvage
```

| | Year | | Accum. Depr. | Exp. | Accum. Depr. | Exp. | Accum. Depr. | Exp. | Accum. Depr. |
Description	Acquired	Cost	12/31/88	1989	12/31/89	1990	12/31/90	1991	12/31/91
BUILDING	1986	1,250,000	75,000	25,000	100,000	25,000	125,000		
TRUCKS/CARS									
Trucks (2)	1986	25,000	21,875	1,562	23,437	0	23,437		
Auto (1)	1986	8,000	7,000	500	7,500	0			
Trucks (2)	1987	28,000	21,000	3,500	24,500	1,750	26,250		
Autos (2)	1987	15,000	11,250	1,875	13,125	937	14,062		
Trucks (2)	1988	30,000	15,000	7,500	22,500	3,750	26,250		
Autos (2)	1988	20,000	10,000	5,000	15,000	2,500	17,500		
Balance 12/31/88		126,000	86,125						
Truck (1)	1989	18,000		9,000	9,000	4,500	13,500		
Auto (1)	1986	(8,000)			(7,500)				
Balance 12/31/89		136,000		28,937	107,562				
Trucks (2)	1990	38,000				19,000	19,000		
Trucks (2)	1986	(25,000)					(23,437)		
Autos (2)	1990	24,000				12,000	12,000		
Balance 12/31/90		173,000				44,437	128,562	0	0
WAREHOUSE EQUIPMENT									
Fork Lift trucks (2)	1986	20,000	7,500	2,500	10,000	2,500	12,500		
Balance 12/31/90		20,000				2,500	12,500	0	0
OFFICE EQUIPMENT									
Various	1986	31,000	18,600	6,200	24,800	6,200	31,000		
Various	1987	5,000	2,000	1,000	3,000	1,000	4,000		
Various	1988	27,500	5,500	5,500	11,000	5,500	16,500		
Bal. 12/31/88		63,500	26,100						
Furniture	1989	1,000		200	200	200	400		
Bal. 12/31/89		64,500		12,900	39,000				
Various	1990	2,500				500	500		
Bal. 12/31/90		67,000				13,400	52,400	0	0
LEASE	1990	550,366							

```
F  = Footed all columns (Initial _____)
CF = Cross-footed all columns (Initial _____)
V  = Verified all computations (Initial _____)
```

Assignment 6

Systems Direct
Repairs and Maintenance (PBC)
December 31, 1990

File name: repairs
Cells used: a1.f54

General Ledger Account:

Date	Ref.	Debit	Credit
1/31	CD	550	
2/28	CD	550	
3/31	CD	2,750	
4/30	CD	2,350	
5/31	CD	825	
6/30	CD	725	
7/31	CD	550	
8/31	CD	875	
9/30	CD	2,450	
10/31	CD	850	
11/30	CD	2,300	
12/31	CD	675	
12/31	GJ	3,300	

Balance per trial balance 18,750

Balance per audit

Analysis:

Building Repairs, Inc. painting office	3,300	E
Janitorial service 250/month	2,750	E
Trash removal 300/month	3,300	E
Detroit Drapes-new drapes for offices	2,200	E
Commercial Refrigeration Service		
Rep. and service air cond. system	1,800	E
Pete's Plumbers - repair and service	950	E
Forklift Service, Inc.		
major overhaul two fork lift trucks	4,000	E (1)
Various - none over $ 50	450	

Totals 18,750

(1) Does not extend life. Amortize over four years.

Audit adjustments:

E = Examined underlying invoices

```
Systems Direct                              File name:   fixasset
Fixed Asset Acquisitions & Dispositions     Cells used:  a1.g47
December 31, 1990
```

Trucks and Cars:
July 18   Purchased two 1990 trucks from Suburban
           Motors, Inc.
           List price (see copy of invoice)   46,000
           Less trade-in allowance   (8,000)

           Cash paid   38,000 T
                                                                    ======

           The fair market value of the trucks traded
           was $5,000.

           Client recorded this transaction as follows:
                 220 Trucks and Cars   38,000
                 221 Accum. Depr. - Trucks & Cars   23,437
                 825 Loss - Disposal of Fixed Assets   1,563
                 101   Cash in Bank - Regular   38,000
                 220   Trucks and Cars   25,000

Sept. 8   Purchased two Corollo sedans from Motown
           Motors, Inc.
           List price (see copy of invoice)   24,000 T
                                                                    ======

           No trade-ins

Office Equipment:
Aug. 24   Purchased ten file cabinets and two desks from
           Metal Case, Inc. (invoice attached)   2,500 T
                                                                     =====

Audit adjustment:

T= Traced to payments in check register
E= Examined underlying invoices

Assignment 6   115

INVOICE

Suburban Motors, Inc.
116 Cross Street
Detroit, Michigan

DATE: July 18, 1990

SOLD TO: Systems Direct
123 State Street
Detroit, Michigan

DELIVER TO: Same

Terms: 2/10/N30   F.O.B. SHIPPING POINT

QUANTITY	DESCRIPTION	UNIT COST	TOTAL COST
2	1988 Trucks – V8	$23,000	$46,000
	Less: Trade-in allowance, 2 – 1984 Trucks		8,000

RECEIVED V.V. 7/20/90

Thank You

FREIGHT
TOTAL – BALANCE DUE $38,000

Motown Motors
102 Jefferson Drive
Detroit, Michigan

INVOICE

SOLD TO: Systems Direct
123 State Street
Detroit, Michigan

SHIP TO: Same

DATE: Sept. 8, 1990

Terms: 2/10/N30   F.O.B. SHIPPING POINT

QUANTITY	DESCRIPTION	UNIT COST	TOTAL COST
2	Corollo Sedans		$24,000

RECEIVED V.V. 9/10/90

FREIGHT
TOTAL – BALANCE DUE $24,000

Thank You

INVOICE

Metal Case Office Equipment, Inc.
703 River Street
Grand Rapids, Michigan

DATE: Aug. 24, 1990

SOLD TO: Systems Direct
123 State Street
Detroit, Michigan

DELIVER TO: Same

Terms: 2/10/N30   F.O.B. SHIPPING POINT

QUANTITY	DESCRIPTION	UNIT COST	TOTAL COST
10	File Cabinets	$150	$1,500
2	Desks	375	750

RECEIVED e.m. 8/26/90

Thank You

TOTAL MERCHANDISE $2,250
FREIGHT 250
TOTAL – BALANCE DUE $2,500

Assignment 6   117

Systems Direct
Lease Calculations
December 31, 1990

File name: leaseanl
Cells used: a1.g55

Audit notes:
A copy of the lease is included in the permanent file.
The lease has been deemed to be a capital lease and, accordingly, should be capitalized along with the obligation under the lease at the company's cost of capital rate.
No amortization should be taken in 1990 since operations at the leased facility will not begin until January, 1991.

Monthly amortization of the lease for 1991 for recurring monthly entries may be computed on the straight-line basis.

This schedule also appears in the long-term liability workpapers.

Lease   (Note: This is an annuity due.)

    Present value of deferred payments:

    Basis of Lease   18,000

    Balance per trial balance

    Difference AJE_____
                                                                =========

Lease Obligation

    PV at 10/1/90   - per above
    PV at 12/1/90   @PV(   )

    Reduction in principal in 1990
                                                     =========

    Long-term portion of L/T debt:
    PV at 12/1/91 @PV(   )

    Current portion of L/T debt   AJE 35
                                                     =========

Accrued Interest at 12/31/90

                                                     =========

    Accrued interest (   )   (AJE __)
                                                   =========

Audit adjustments:

ASSIGNMENT 7

OTHER CURRENT LIABILITIES

(Accounts Payable - Other, Accrued Salaries and Bonuses, Interest, Payroll, Income Taxes, Pension Obligation, and Dividends)

AUDIT PROGRAM

Summary of assignments:

Review January check register for unrecorded liabilities.

Trace payments for recorded liabilities to January check register.

Calculate additional business license liability based on actual sales for the year.

Prepare entries to adjust liabilities for accrued bonuses, interest, and income taxes.

General

Initial Date

1. Foot and crossfoot lead schedule and all other PBC schedules. ____ ____

2. Compare balances on other PBC schedules with balances on the lead schedule. ____ ____

3. Compare balances on lead schedule with account balances in the trial balance. ____ ____

Analytical Review Procedures

1. Review entries to these accounts for the period and investigate large or unusual items. *DHW* ____

2. Review minutes for authorization for:
   a. Dividend declaration ____ ____
   b. Bonuses ____ ____

Other Substantive Audit Procedures

Accounts Payable - Other

1. Review January check register for additional December liabilities not included above ____ ____

2. Prepare adjusting journal entry, if necessary. ____ ____

Initial Date

Current Portion - Long-Term Debt

1. Prepare entry to reclassify current portion of mortgage payable. (To be completed after Assignment 8.) ____ ____

Lease Obligation - Current

1. Prepare entry to reclassify current portion of lease. (To be completed after Assignment 8. ____ ____

Pension Obligation

1. Examine supporting documentation. *DHW* ____

2. Vouch payments made during the year to the pension trustee. *DHW* ____

3. Verify that total employee benefits do not exceed 15% of total salaries and bonuses paid during the year. ____ ____

4. Trace payment of 12/31 liability to January check register, making appropriate notes as indicated on the workpaper. ____ ____

5. Prepare a footnote to accompany financial statements. ____ ____

Accrued Expenses (Salaries, Interest, Bonuses)

1. Examine supporting documentation. *DHW* ____

2. Record in this file adjusting journal entries made during audit of other accounts (i.e., payroll, additional business license accrual, interest on lease obligation, bonus accruals). (Cannot be completed until after Assignment 8.) ____ ____

3. Review January check register to determine if any other accruals are required. ____ ____

Payroll Taxes Withheld and Accrued

1. Compare salaries reported with employee earnings cards, payrolls, and general ledger salary accounts

and payroll tax returns filed during the year.   *DHW* ___

2. Verify deductions with authorizations in personnel records (i.e., number of exemptions, other payroll deductions.   *DHW* ___

3. On a test basis, compare endorsements on checks to signatures in personnel file.   *DHW* ___

4. Compare total wages and deductions on employee earnings cards to end-of-year W-2 statements filed with the IRS.   *DHW* ___

5. Mail employees' W-2 copies to employees' home addresses in our envelopes.   *DHW* ___

6. Trace payment of 12/31 liability to January check register, making appropriate notes as indicated on the workpaper.   ___ ___

Income Tax Payable

1. Examine quarterly estimated tax returns, entries in the check register, canceled checks and postings to the account.   *DHW* ___

2. Trace postings from the recurring general journal to the account.   *DHW* ___

Note: The remaining portions of this assignment cannot be completed until after Assignment 8.

3. Post all adjusting entries to the work sheet.   ___ ___

4. Complete workpaper calculation of total income tax expense for the year, income tax payable and deferred income taxes.   ___ ___

5. Prepare adjusting journal entry.   ___ ___

6. Prepare appropriate footnote to the financial statements on accounting policies.   ___ ___

Dividends Payable

See audit procedures for stockholder's equity.

Deferred Income Tax

See audit procedures for income taxes.

Note: See long-term liability workpapers for current maturities on long-term debt.

Required:

1. Complete the audit program to the extent possible.

2. Complete the lead schedule to the extent possible. (Entries still needed for bonus and income accruals, and reclassification entries for current maturities of long-term debt.)

3. Turn in the following in the order listed:

   a. Time budget

   b. Audit program

   c. Lead schedule

   d. Adjusting entries with explanations

   e. Pension obligation

   f. Payroll taxes withheld and accrued workpaper

   g. Accounts Payable—Other

   h. Accrued expenses

   i. Salaries expense, employee benefits, payroll tax expense

Note: Your instructor may want you to hold the above until you have completed Assignment 8 and submit both at the same time.

Systems Direct
Other Current Liabilities Lead Schedule (PBC)
December 31, 1990

File name: curllead
Cells used: a1.h39

Acct. No.	Account Title	Per T/B	#	Adjustments Dr.	#	Cr.	Per Audit
301	Accounts Payable - Other	(3,300)					
310	Current Portion - Long-term Debt	0					
311	Lease Obligation - Current	0					
312	Pension Obligation	(15,908)					
320	Accrued Expenses - Salaries, Interest and Bonuses	(132,579)					
330	Payroll Taxes - Withheld & Accrued	(13,306)					
335	Income Taxes Payable	(47,026)					
340	Dividends Payable	(100,000)					
350	Deferred Income Tax	0					
		(312,119)		0		0	0

Audit adjustments:

Assignment 7

```
Systems Direct                          File name:      acpayoth
Accounts Payable - Other (PBC)          Cells used:     a1.h19
December 31, 1990

Building Repairs, Inc. painting offices                    3,300
                                                         -------
        Balance per trial balance                          3,300

Audit adjustments:
```

```
Systems Direct                          File name:      accruexp
Accrued Expenses                        Cells used:     a1.h55
December 31, 1990

Bonuses accrued by client based on monthly
    income statements                                    102,015
Payroll - December 30, 1990                               30,564
                                                         -------
        Balance per trial balance                        132,579

Audit adjustments:                                       -------




        Balance per audit:
                                                        ========
```

Systems Direct
Salaries Expense
Employee Benefits
Payroll Taxes Expense
Years Ended December 31, 1989 and 1990

File name: salpenpr
Cells used: a1.f117

	1989	1990
Salaries and bonuses paid during year:		
(see note at end of file)		
Officers' salaries (Acct. 800)		
President	68,200	75,000
V.P. - Finance	54,500	60,000
V.P. - Administration	54,500	60,000
V.P. - Marketing/Sales	54,500	60,000
Bonuses - Officers	45,954	36,000
Total officers' compensation expense	277,654	291,000
Other salaries (Acct. 801)		
Chief Accountant	36,400	40,000
General Ledger Bookkeeper	22,730	25,000
Accounts Receivable Bookkeeper	15,900	17,500
Accounts Payable Bookkeeper	15,900	17,500
Clerical Staff - Accounting	13,640	15,000
Clerical Staff - Accounting	13,640	15,000
Clerical Staff- Administration	11,365	12,500
Clerical Staff- Administration	11,365	12,500
Warehouse Manager	22,730	25,000
Inventory Manager	18,180	20,000
Warehouse Staff	13,640	15,000
Warehouse Staff	11,365	12,500
Warehouse Staff	11,365	12,500
Clerical Staff- Market/Sales	11,365	12,500
Clerical Staff- Market/Sales	11,365	12,500
Salesperson - A	18,190	20,000
Salesperson - B	18,190	20,000
Salesperson - C	18,190	20,000
Salesperson - D	18,190	20,000
Salesperson - E	18,190	20,000
Bonuses - Salespersons	26,000	66,015
Total compensation - expense - Other	357,900	431,015
Total compensation expense	635,554	722,015
Add: Bonuses paid beginning of year	52,925	71,954
Less: Bonuses accrued end of year	(71,954)	(102,015)
Total compensation paid during year	616,525	691,954
(basis for pension and payroll tax computations)		

(over)

Assignment 7

Employee Benefits - Acct. # 802

Total compensation paid during year	616,525	691,954
15% x total compensation paid	92,479	103,793

Payroll Taxes Expense - Acct. # 803
FICA:

Total compensation paid during year	616,525	691,954
Excess salaries:		
1989 maximum - $ 47,100	43,300	
1990 maximum - $ 49,500		57,000
Taxable FICA salaries	573,225	634,954
FICA Tax Rate	0.0751	0.0765
FICA Tax Expense	43,049	48,574

FUTA:

Total compensation paid during year	616,525	691,954
Excess salaries:		
1989 maximum - $ 7,000	448,525	
1990 maximum - $ 7,000		523,954
Taxable FUTA Salaries	168,000	168,000
FUTA tax rate	0.0620	0.0620
Less maximum credit	0.0540	0.0540
Effective FUTA tax rate	0.0080	0.0080
FUTA Tax Expense	1,344	1,344

SUTA:

Total compensation paid during year	616,525	691,954
Excess salaries:		
1989 maximum - $ 9,500	388,525	
1990 maximum - $ 9,500		463,954
Taxable SUTA Salaries	228,000	228,000
SUTA tax rate (based on employment experience-minimum rate is .01%)	0.0010	0.0010
SUTA Tax Expense	228	228
Total Payroll Tax Expense	44,621	50,146

Note:
Payroll taxes are determined by salaries and bonuses paid, not accrued. We have assumed that this also applies to employee benefits (pensions). Hence, this schedule is necessary to audit the employee benefits and payroll tax expense accounts.

Estimates were used for the wage bases.

T= Traced to payroll check register
V= Calculations verified
F= Footed columns

Systems Direct
Payroll Taxes Withheld and Accrued
December 31, 1990

Payroll taxes withheld and
accrued $13,306

Balance per trial balance $13,306

Assignment:

By reference to January check register, ascertain that payroll taxes withheld and accrued at December 31, 1990, were paid noting the following:

Date of check _____
Check # _____
Amount _____
Initial _____
Date procedure performed _____

AUDIT MEMO

I have reviewed the quarterly payroll tax returns filed by the client and performed the following audit procedures:

1. Compared salaries reported with employee earnings cards, payrolls, and general ledger salary accounts;

2. Verified deductions with authorizations as shown on personnel records, i.e. number of exemptions, etc.

3. On a test basis, compared endorsements on checks to signatures in personnel files.

4. Compared total wages and deductions on employee earnings cards to end-of-year W-2 satements filed with the Internal Revenue Service.

5. Mailed W-2 employees' copies to employees' home addresses in our envelopes.

DHW 1/28/91

Systems Direct
Pension Obligation--Employee Benefits
December 31, 1990

Balance per trial balance - December 31, 1990 $15,908

<u>Memo for Workpapers</u>

The company maintains a pension program for all employees and contributes 100% of the contribution into the plan. Contributions are used to pay premiums on annuities for each employee.

Remittance to the pension trustee is made quarterly and is based on 15% of salaries and bonuses paid during the year.

I have vouched the payments made during the year to the pension trustee.

The balance in the Employee Benefits account is $119,142 and equals 15% of the total salaries and bonuses paid during the year. See schedule of salaries and bonuses paid in workpapers.

DHW 1/5/91

Vouch payment of balance in # 312 to pension trustee in January, 1991, noting the following:

Date of payment _____
Check number _____
Amount _____
Initials _____

Assignment 7

Systems Direct
Bonus and Income Tax Computations
December 31, 1989

This is a copy from last year's workpapers provided to your
firm by Dewitt and Tanner, CPAs, and should serve as a guide for
this year's computations.

Bonus Provisions:
    President - 10% of income after income taxes and all bonuses.
    Vice-President - Marketing/Sales - 5% of income before income taxes
        but after salespersons' bonuses. (Note increase in bonus.)
    Salespersons - 20% of sales, before audit adjustments, in
        excess of quotas.

Net income before bonuses and income taxes   468,482

Bonus Computations:

Salesperson	Quota	Actual	Excess	Bonus	
A	2,100,000	2,150,000	50,000	10,000	
B	1,800,000	1,825,000	25,000	5,000	
C	1,200,000	1,230,000	30,000	6,000	
D	800,000	800,000	0	0	
E	400,000	425,000	25,000	5,000	
House	84,000	84,000	0	0	
Totals	6,384,000	6,514,000	130,000	26,000	(26,000)

Income subject to Vice-President's bonus   442,482
Less bonus - Vice-President (5% x 442,482)   22,124   (22,124)

Income subject to President's bonus   420,358
Less bonus - President (see calculations)   23,794   (23,794)

Accrued bonuses   71,918

Income before income taxes   396,564
Income tax expense (40% x 396,564)   (158,626)

Net income   237,938

Calculation - President's bonus and income taxes:
Let B = President's bonus
    T = Income taxes

Then: B = .1 (420,358 - B - T)
      T = .4 (420,358 - B)

      B = 42,036 - .1B - .1T
      T = 168,143 - .4B

      B = 42,036 - .1B - .1(168,143 - .4B)
      B = 25,225 - .06B
      B = 23,794

      T = .4(420,358 - 23,794)
      T = 158,626

Systems Direct
Bonus and Income Tax Calculations
December 31, 1990

File name: bonustax
Cells used: a1.h134

Bonus provisions:
  President - 10% of income after income taxes and all bonuses
  V. P. Marketing/Sales - 10% of income before income taxes,
    but after salespersons' bonuses
  Salespersons' - 20% of sales in excess of quotas

Audit note:
Before computing bonuses and income taxes, post the adjusting journal entries to the worksheet; extend and complete the worksheet arriving at a credit balance in the income statement column. This represents income after monthly bonus and income tax accruals made by the client. To this figure add back the monthly accruals to arrive at the income before bonuses and income taxes. Then complete this worksheet using last year's as a guide.

Income after monthly bonus and income tax
    accruals   (From trial balance worksheet)
Add back:
  Monthly bonus accruals:
    Officers   36,000
    Salespersons   66,015   102,015

  Monthly income tax accruals   207,026

Income before bonuses and income taxes

BONUS COMPUTATIONS:
Salespersons:

Name	Quota	Actual	Excess	Bonus
A	2,500,000	2,600,000		
B	2,100,000	2,250,000		
C	1,400,000	1,500,000		
D	875,000	875,000		
E	500,000	550,000		
House(1)	94,222	94,222		
Totals	7,469,222	7,869,222	400,000	80,000

(1) No bonus on house sales

Income subject to officers' bonuses   0
Bonus - V.P. Marketing/Sales:
        (10% x   )

Income subject to president's bonus   0
Bonus - President:
         (see calculation)
                                                  --------- ---------
Income before income taxes   0
                                                           =========

Total bonuses   0
Less: previously accrued   (102,015)

Additional bonus accrual
                                                 =========

Assignment 7   127

	Total	Officers # 800	Other # 801
Additional bonus allocated as follows:			
Total bonuses per above			
Less: previously paid	(102,015)	(36,000)	(66,015)
Additional bonus accrual			

Income before income taxes (above)

Income Tax Expense - (See calculations - next page)
Less: Deferred income taxes on installment sales
     See Notes Receivable workpapers

Income Tax Payable
Less: Previously paid on estimates
     See Income Tax Payable workpaper

Remaining income tax payable

Income Tax Expense (above)
Balance per trial balance acct. # 830

Reduction in Income Tax Expense account

Bonus and Tax Calculations

Let B = President's bonus
    T = Income tax expense

Audit adjustment:

128   Assignment 7

Systems Direct
Income Taxes Payable (PBC)
December 31, 1990

File name: inctxpay
Cells used: a1.i44

DHW prepared the following analysis.

		Dr.	Cr.
Balance - December 31, 1989			40,006
3/11/90 paid balance	CD	40,006 E	
4/15/90 paid 1st qtr.'90 estimate	CD	40,000 E	
6/15/90 paid 2nd qtr.'90 estimate	CD	40,000 E	
9/15/90 paid 3rd qtr.'90 estimate	CD	40,000 E	
12/15/90 paid 4th qtr.'90 estimate	CD	40,000 E	
Cumulative credits from eleven monthly recurring general journal entries based on monthly income statements.	RGJ		207,026 T
		200,006	247,032
			200,006
Balance per trial balance			47,026

Audit adjustment:

Balance per audit - December 31, 1990

Check:
Total income tax payable (excluding deferred)
    from tax and bonus calculation
Less: previously paid (above)   160,000

Remaining income tax due   0
                                                      =========

E = Examined cancelled check and estimated tax returns
T = Traced postings from recurring general journal to
    general ledger account
T/B = Agrees with trial balance

Assignment 7

```
Systems Direct                      File name:    dividend
Dividends Payable                   Cells used:   a1.f15
December 31, 1990


Balance per trial balance                         100,000
                                                  ========


Audit notes:
    Reviewed minutes for authorization. _____
    Verified calculation of amount of dividend. _____
    Date procedures were performed. _____
    Initials _____
```

ASSIGNMENT 8

LONG-TERM LIABILITIES

AUDIT PROGRAM

Summary of assignment:

Verify mortgage calculations for principal and interest, prepare entry to adjust unpaid principal, and record interest expense.

Reclassify current portion of principal.

Calculate lease, lease obligation, and interest, and prepare adjusting entry.

Reclassify current portion of lease.

Analyze interest expense.

Prepare appropriate footnotes for financial statements.

General

                                                             Initial   Date

1. Foot and crossfoot lead schedule and all other PBC schedules. _____ _____

2. Compare balances on other PBC schedule(s) with balances on lead schedule. _____ _____

3. Compare balances on lead schedule with account balances in the trial balance. _____ _____

Analytical Review Procedures

1. Review entries to these accounts for the period, and trace to source journals and underlying documentation. *DHW* _____

2. Review entries to related interest expense accounts. *DHW* _____

3. Confirm debt. (See bank confirmation.) *DHW* _____

Other Substantive Audit Procedures

Mortgage Payable

1. Review clerical accuracy of carrying value of long-term debt and related interest expense accounts. _____ _____

                                                             Initial   Date

2. Verify proper amount of current portion of long-term liabilities and prepare reclassification journal entry. _____ _____

3. Review for proper financial statement classification and disclosure. Prepare notes to financial statements. _____ _____

Lease Obligation

1. Examine supporting documentation. (See copy of lease in permanent file.) _____ _____

2. Review minutes for proper authorization. _____ _____

3. Calculate carrying value of lease obligation and (Refer to Assignment 6.) _____ _____

4. Calculate interest expense. _____ _____

5. Prepare appropriate adjusting journal entry. _____ _____

6. Prepare reclassification entry to show current portion as a current liability. _____ _____

7. Prepare appropriate footnote to the financial statements. _____ _____

Required:

1. Complete the audit program.
2. Complete the lead schedule.
3. Turn in the following in the order listed:
   a. Time budget
   b. Audit program
   c. Lead schedule
   d. Adjusting entries with explanations
   e. Mortgage payable workpaper
   f. Lease calculations workpaper
   g. Interest expense and payable workpaper

Systems Direct
Long-Term Liabilities Lead Schedule (PBC
December 31, 1990

File name: ltllead
Cells used: a1.h26

Acct. No.	Account Title	Per T/B	#	Adjustments Debit	#	Credit	Per Audit
400	Mortgage Payable	(965,742)					
412	Lease Obligation	0					
310	Current Portion - Mortgage Payable	0					
311	Current Portion - Lease Obligation	0					
816	Interest Expense	97,030					

Audit adjustments:

Systems Direct
Mortgage Payable
December 31, 1990

File name: mortpay
Cells used: a1.h42

Balance per trial balance - December 31, 1988   965,742 *
Current portion

Long-term portion
                                                       =======

Audit notes:
The building was acquired 1/1/86, at a cost of $1,250,000. The
company paid $250,000 down and financed the balance with a mortgage
in the amount of $1,000,000, payable monthly over thirty years at an
interest rate of 10%. The mortgagee is Suburban National Bank.

Monthly payments are $8,776, and are allocated between principal and
interest as indicated by the following notes from the permanent file.
Payments are due at the end of each month.

	Payments	Interest	Principal	Balance
January 1, 1986				1,000,000
December 31, 1986	105,312	99,750	5,562	994,438
December 31, 1987	105,312	99,167	6,145	988,293
December 31, 1988	105,312	98,523	6,789	981,504
December 31, 1989	105,312	97,813	7,499	974,005
December 31, 1990	105,312	97,028	8,284	965,721 *
December 31, 1991	105,312	96,160	9,152	956,569

Assignment:
You are to verify the accuracy of the above schedule and of the 1989
and 1990 allocation between principal and interest. Do not adjust the
client's records for a small insignificant difference. Also verify
the accuracy of the interest expense account.

For financial statement purposes, prepare the adjusting journal entry
to transfer the current portion of the principal from account #400
to account #310.

Audit adjustment(s):

* = Ignore minor difference.

```
Systems Direct                      File name:  leaseanl
Lease Calculations                  Cells used: a1.g55
December 31, 1990
```

Audit notes:
A copy of the lease is included in the permanent file.
The lease has been deemed to be a capital lease and,
accordingly, should be capitalized along with the
obligation under the lease at the company's cost of capital
rate.
No amortization should be taken in 1990 since operations
at the leased facility will not begin until January, 1991.

Monthly amortization of the lease for 1991 for recurring
monthly entries may be computed on the straight-line
basis.

This schedule also appears in the fixed asset
workpapers.

Lease   (Note: This is an annuity due.)

    Present value of deferred payments:

    Basis of Lease   18,000

    Balance per trial balance

    Difference AJE_____
                                          =========

Lease Obligation

    PV at 10/1/90   - per above
    PV at 12/1/90   @PV(   )

    Reduction in principal in 1990
                                      =========

    Long-term portion of L/T debt:
    PV at 12/1/91 @PV(   )

    Current portion of L/T debt   AJE 35
                                      =========

Accrued Interest at 12/31/90

                                      =========
    Accrued interest (   )   (AJE __)
                                      =========

Audit adjustments:

```
Systems Direct                          File name:   interest
Interest Expense                        Cells used:  a1.g15
Interest Payable
December 31, 1990


Balance per trial balance - December 31, 1990            97,030

Audit adjustments:


                                                         -------
        Balance per audit
                                                         =======
```

Assignment 8

ASSIGNMENT 9

STOCKHOLDERS' EQUITY

AUDIT PROGRAM

Summary of assignment:

Verify dividend authorization and calculation.

Review analysis of Miscellaneous Expense account.

Review comment on Other Income.

General

                                            Initial   Date

1. Foot lead schedule and all other PBC schedules.

2. Compare balances on other PBC schedules with balances on the lead schedule.

3. Compare balances on lead schedule with account balances in the trial balance.

Analytical Review Procedures

Stockholder's Equity Accounts

1. Compare list of stockholders with stocks in stock certificate book noting dates issued, certificate numbers, number of shares, and in whose name the certificates were issued.   *DHW*

2. Trace proceeds received from issuance of stock to prior year's cash receipts records.   *DHW*

                                            Initial   Date

3. Review minutes for authorization to declare dividends and recompute amount of dividends declared and/or paid.

4. Compute earnings per share to be used in financial statements.

Miscellaneous Expense Account

1. Examine underlying documentation in excess of $50.   *DHW*

2. Post adjusting journal entries, if any, and complete workpaper.

Other Income

1. Review comment on other income in workpapers.

Required:

1. Complete the audit program.
2. Complete the lead schedule.
3. Turn in the following in the order listed:

   a. Time budget

   b. Audit program

   c. Lead schedule

   d. Adjusting entries, if any, with complete explanations

   e. Miscellaneous Expense and comments on Other Income

   f. Completed working trial balance

Systems Direct
Stockholders' Equity Lead Schedule (PBC)
December 31, 1990

File name: skeqlead
Cells used: a1.d30

	Capital Stock #500	Additional Paid-in Capital #510	Retained Earnings #520
Balance - January 1, 1988	100,000	250,000	396,708
Add: Net income - 1988			179,945
Less: Dividends declared			(100,000)
Balance - December 31, 1988	100,000	250,000	476,653
Add: Net income - 1989			237,938
Less: Dividends declared			(100,000)
Balance - December 31, 1989	100,000	250,000	614,591
Add:			
Less:			
Balance - December 31, 1990			

Assignment 9

```
Systems Direct                          File name:    stkhold
Stockholders' Equity                    Cells used:   a1.f16
December 31, 1990
```

Stockholder	Cert. Number	Date Issued	Number of Shares	Amount Paid In
Curtis Jackson	SD 1001	7-1-82	250	87,500
Julie Medina	SD 1002	7-1-82	250	87,500
Diane Smith	SD 1003	7-1-82	250	87,500
Daniel Darrow	SD 1004	7-1-82	250	87,500
Totals			1,000	350,000

Note: Only 1/10 of authorized shares have been issued.

```
Systems Direct                              File name:  miscell
Miscellaneous and Other Expense Accounts    Cells used: a1.h38
December 31, 1990


Balance per trial balance - December 31, 1990                  23,410

Audit adjustment:
                                                              -------
Balance per audit
                                                              =======

Audit notes:
Examined invoices and other evidence in support of charges to this
account in excess of $50. There were some minor discrepancies and
was unable to locate supporting documentation for several charges,
but these are considered immaterial and no adjustment was made.

                                          DHW  1/28/91


The following expense accounts were analyzed in a similar
manner and, accordingly, need no further attention

        805 - Advertising and promotion
        807 - Delivery expenses
        818 - Office supplies expense
        822 - Telephone expense       (1)
        823 - Travel and entertainment
        824 - Utilities      (1)

While not analyzed in detail, we scanned account #620, Other
Income, and found that as last year, the only credits to the
account come from the cash receipts journal and represent
cash received from the sales of scrap wood from overseas
shipping crates of computers and electronic sound equipment.

(1) Each of these accounts contained twelve monthly payments.
```

Assignment 9   139

ASSIGNMENT 10

COMPLETING THE AUDIT

CHECKLIST

Summary of assignment:

This is the lengthiest assignment to complete.

The assignment essentially wraps up the audit and involves the following activities:

- Completing the working trial balance and the AJE file
- Indexing the workpapers
- Preparing and obtaining the representation letters
- Preparing financial statements and footnotes
- Computing selected ratios
- Preparing monthly recurring journal entries for next year

General

		Initial	Date
1.	Review for subsequent events.	DHW	___
2.	Extend audit procedures sufficiently to permit an opinion as to consistency.	DHW	___
3.	Review workpapers for:		
	a. Any open or unresolved matters	___	___
	b. Completeness of comments, conclusions, calculations, AJE explanations, etc.	___	___
	c. Proper headings and dates	___	___
4.	Prepare representation letters:		
	a. From management	___	___
	b. From attorney	DHW	___
5.	Index workpapers. (Ask your instructor as to firm policy.)	___	___
6.	Prepare 1991 monthly recurring general journal entries for client.	___	___

		Initial	Date
7.	Prepare audit report:		
	a. Income Statement	___	___
	b. Statement of Retained Earnings	___	___
	c. Balance Sheet	___	___
	d. Statement of Cash Flows (following new format per SFAS #95)	___	___
	e. Notes to Financial Statements	___	___
	f. Audit Report	___	___
8.	Compute the ratios shown on the ratio schedule and compare with those of the preceding year, noting any unusual changes.	___	___

Required:

1. Complete the audit program.
2. Turn in the following in the order listed:

Group I

Time budget

Audit program for Assignment 10

Group II

Income statement

Balance Sheet

Statement of Retained Earnings

Statement of Cash Flows (**Note:** All statements should be comparative with prior year.)

Notes to Financial Statements

Auditor's Report

Group III

Recurring journal entries—for next year

Computation of selected ratios

Management Letter—including internal control weaknesses from Assignment 1 plus any additional weaknesses observed during the audit

Completed working trial balance

```
Systems Direct                            File name:   aje
Adjusting Journal Entries                 Cells used:  a1.
December 31, 1990

 Acct.
  No.           Account Title              Debit       Credit
 -----  ---------------------------------  -------    --------
                    AJE 1
```

Assignment 10

MANAGEMENT REPRESENTATION LETTER

Assignment:

Included below is a generic list of items usually included in a management representation letter, taken from Section AU 333.04 of Statements on Auditing Standards.

Your assignment is to reword the appropriate sections into the form of a letter, dated March 5, 1991, addressed to Smith & Weiss, CPAs, and signed by President Jackson of Systems Direct. It would appear that item i. is the only item not applicable to this audit. Accordingly, your letter should make reference to each item a. through t., omitting i.

You may wish to consult your text for guidance in how to group these items into letter form.

OBTAINING WRITTEN REPRESENTATIONS

<u>AU 333.04</u>   The specific written representations obtained by the auditor will depend on the circumstances of the engagement and the nature and basis of presentation of the financial statements.
They ordinarily include the following matters, if applicable:

a. Management's acknowledgment of its responsibility for the fair presentation in the financial statements of financial position, results of operations, and changes in financial position in conformity with generally accepted accounting principles or other comprehensive basis of accounting.

b. Availability of all financial records and related data.

c. Completeness and availability of all minutes of meetings of stockholders, directors, and committees of directors.

d. Absence of errors in the financial statements and unrecorded transactions.

e. Information concerning related party transactions and related amounts receivable or payable.

f. Noncompliance with aspects of contractual agreements that may affect the financial statements.

g. Information concerning subsequent events.

h. Irregularities involving management or employees.

i. N/A Communications from regulatory agencies concerning non-compliance with, or deficiencies in, financial reporting practices.

j. Plans or intentions that may affect the carrying value or classification of assets or liabilities.

k. Disclosure of compensating balances or other arrangements involving restrictions on cash balances, and disclosure of line-of-credit or similar arrangements.

l. Reduction of excess or obsolete inventories to net realizable value.

m. Losses from sales commitments.

n. Satisfactory title to assets, liens on assets, and assets pledged as collateral.

o. Agreements to repurchase assets previously sold.

p. Losses from purchase commitments for inventory quantities in excess of requirements or at prices in excess of market.

q. Violations or possible violations of laws or regulations whose effects should be considered for disclosure in the financial statements or as a basis for recording a loss contingency.

r. Other liabilities and gain or loss contingencies that are required to be accrued or disclosed by Statement of Financial Accounting Standards No. 5 [AC section C59].

s. Unasserted claims or assessments that the client's lawyer has advised are probable of assertion and must be disclosed in accordance with Statement of Financial Accounting Standards No. 5 [AC section C59].

t. Capital stock repurchase options or agreements or capital stock reserved for options, warrants, conversions, or other requirements.

Source: Auditing Standards Board, AU333.04

SYSTEMS DIRECT

123 State Street
Detroit, Michigan

Brown and Beaver, Attorneys at Law
76 Court Street Detroit, Michigan

January 4, 1991

Dear Sir or Madam:

In connection with and examination of our financial statements at December 31, 1990 and for the year then ended, management of the Company has prepared, and furnished to our auditors, Smith & Weiss, CPAs, Detroit, MI, a description and evaluation of certain contingencies, including those set forth below involving matters with respect to which you have been engaged and to which you have devoted substantive attention on behalf of the Company in the form of legal consultation or representation. These contingencies are regarded by management of the Company as material for this purpose. Your response should include matters that existed at December 31, 1990 and during the period from that date to the date of your response.

Pending or Threatened Litigation (excluding unasserted claims)

Please furnish to our auditors such explanation, if any, that you consider necessary to supplement the foregoing information, including an explanation of those matters as to which your views may differ from those stated and an identification of the omission of any pending or threatened litigation, claims, and assessments or a statement that the list of such matters is complete.

Unasserted Claims and Assessments (considered by management to be probable of assertion, and that, if asserted, would have at least a reasonable possibility of an unfavorable outcome)

Please furnish our auditors such explanation, if any, that you consider necessary to supplement the foregoing information, including an explanation of those matters as to which your views may differ from those stated.

We understand that whenever, in the course of performing legal services for us with respect to a matter recognized to involve an unasserted possible claim or assessment that may call for financial statement disclosure, if you have formed a professional conclusion that we should disclose or consider disclosure concerning such possible claim or assessment and, as a matter of professional responsibility to us, you will so advise us and will consult with us concerning such possible claim or assessment, as a matter of professional responsibility to us, you will so advise us and will consult with us concerning the question of such disclosure and the applicable requirements of Statement of Financial Accounting Standards No. 5. Please specifically confirm to our auditors that our understanding is correct.

Please specifically identify the nature of and reasons for any limitation on your response.

Sincerely,
Systems Direct

C. Jackson
C. Jackson, President

Source: Auditing Standards Board, AU 337A.01

ATTORNEY'S LETTER

BROWN AND BEAVER
Attorneys at Law

76 Court Street
Detroit, Michigan

Smith & Weiss, CPAs
January 10, 1991
Detroit, Michigan

Ladies and Gentlemen:

This is in response to your letter dated January 4, 1991, in regard to your audit of the financial statements of Systems Direct.

We have served as general counsel to Systems Direct since the corporation was formed and operations began. In this regard, I advise you that during the year under audit we have not counseled Systems Direct regarding potential litigation nor is there any pending litigation at December 31, 1990. Furthermore, our firm is not aware of any material loss contingencies and/or unasserted claims or assessments within the requirements of Statement of Financial Accounting Standards No. 5.

If we can be of further service, please let us know.

Sincerely,

R. Beaver

Brown and Beaver
Attorneys at Law

As part of your audit as well as a service to management your firm computes certain selected ratios which, together with comments thereon, are to be included as an appendix to your management letter.

There are two basic reasons for computing ratios at the conclusion of an audit; first, ratio analysis is an analytical review procedure designed to highlight inconsistencies and/or significant changes which may result from errors in the input data, i.e., receivables, inventories, etc., thus serving as a reasonableness test. Also, the auditor has an obligation to alert the client to unfavorable trends as may be indicated by a series of ratios covering several periods.

To save time at the conclusion of the audit the worksheet on the following pages has been prepared in skeletal form awaiting the final figures at the completion of the audit.

You are to do the following:

1. Compute the ratios indicated by referring to the current financial statements and those of the predecessor auditors;

2. Comment on any significant trends or unusual changes that you feel should be brought to the attention of management.

```
Systems Direct                          File name:   ratio
Selected Ratios                         Cells used:  a1.m77
December 31, 1990
                            1990                 1989                 1988
                         $ Amount    Ratio    $ Amount    Ratio    $ Amount    Ratio
                        ----------- ------   ----------- ------   ----------- ------

PROFITABILITY RATIOS
  Gross Profit Margin:
    Gross Profit
    ------------         ----------- =       ----------- =        ----------- =
      Net Sales


  Net Income to Sales:
    Net Income
    ----------           ----------- =       ----------- =        ----------- =
     Net Sales


  Return on Equity:
      Net Income
   --------------------  ----------- =       ----------- =        ----------- =
   Stockholders' Equity
      (Beg. of year)


  Return on Total Assets:
      Net Income
   ------------------    ----------- =       ----------- =        ----------- =
    Total Assets (Beg.)                                            2,175,000
```

Assignment 10   145

	1990 $ Amount	Ratio	1989 $ Amount	Ratio	1988 $ Amount	Ratio

LIQUIDITY RATIOS
  Current Ratio:
    Current Assets
    ------------------   ----------- =   ----------- =   ----------- =
    Current Liabilities

  Quick (Acid Test) Ratio:
    Cash + Acct. Rec.(net)
    ----------------------   ----------- =   ----------- =   ----------- =
    Current Liabilities

OPERATING CYCLE RATIOS:
  Accts. Rec. Turnover:
    Net Sales
    ------------------   ----------- =   ----------- =   ----------- =
    Average Accts. Rec.
      (See below)

  Avg. Accts. Rec. (Gross):
    Beginning   706,140
    Ending
    Average (/2)

  Inventory Turnover:
    Cost of Sales
    ------------------   ----------- =   ----------- =   ----------- =
    Average Inventory
      (See below)

  Avg. Inventory:
    Beginning   251,146
    Ending
    Average (/2)

  No. of Days in Oper. Cycle:
  Days in inventory   365/   =   365/   =   365/   =
  Days in receivable   365/   =   365/   =   365/   =
                                           ---   ---   ---
  Days in operating cycle   0   0   0
                                           ===   ===   ===

SOLVENCY (DEBT/EQUITY):
    Total Liabilities
    -----------------   ----------- =   ----------- =   ----------- =
    Total Assets

Comments on selected ratios are included in the management letter and are not repeated here.

146   Assignment 10

Systems Direct
Recurring Monthly General Journal Entries
For 1991

File name: rgj91
Cells used: a1.d46

Acct. No.	Accounts	Debit	Credit
Depreciation expenses:			
810	Building	2,083	
211	Accum. Depr. - Building		2,083
811	Trucks and Cars	2,400	
221	Accum. Depr. - Trucks and Cars		2,400
812	Warehouse Equipment	208	
231	Accum. Depr. - Warehouse Equipment		208
813	Office Equipment	1,075	
241	Accum. Depr. - Office Equipment		1,075
250	Lease		
251	Accum. Amortization - Lease		
806	Bad Debt Expense	9,000	
121	Allowance for Doubtful Accounts		9,000
	(/12)		
815	Insurance Expense	2,000	
140	Prepaid Expense		2,000
	(/12)		
800	Salaries and Bonuses - Officers	Various	
801	Salaries and Bonuses - Other	Various	
320	Accrued Expenses		Various
802	Employee Benefits	Various	
312	Pension Obligation		Various
819	Professional Expenses	2,600	
140	Prepaid Expenses		2,600
	(/12)		
822	Taxes and Licenses	6,000	
140	Prepaid Expenses		6,000
	(/12)		
830	Income Tax Expense	Various	
335	Income Tax Payable		Various

LOTUS 1-2-3 TUTORIAL

This tutorial consists of four lessons that are designed to acquaint you with the Lotus 1-2-3 program. Each lesson will take about 45 minutes to complete. You may wish to work the tutorial before attempting any of the problems in the workbook. If you have worked through any other workbook from this ELECTRONIC SPREADSHEET APPLICATIONS SERIES, you may proceed directly to the problems and use the tutorial as a reference.

This tutorial is not written to teach you in-depth Lotus 1-2-3 programming. Its purpose is to expose you to the basic elements of 1-2-3 and prepare you to solve the problems in this workbook. You are strongly encouraged to explore more advanced 1-2-3 programming on your own after completing this tutorial. You can learn about 1-2-3 in more detail from the Lotus 1-2-3 manual that accompanies the Lotus 1-2-3 program. There are numerous reference materials available on 1-2-3 in many bookstores and computer stores. There is also a computer-programmed Tutorial Disk for 1-2-3 that comes with the Lotus program. It is a self-paced instructional program that provides a nice introduction to the many features of 1-2-3.

Lotus 1-2-3 is called an electronic spreadsheet. What exactly is an electronic spreadsheet? Imagine a large sheet of accounting paper with many columns and rows. In the business world this is often referred to as a worksheet or spreadsheet. Spreadsheets are commonly used to gather financial data and to accumulate the results. Electronic spreadsheets are computer programs that are similar to paper spreadsheets in structure and format. One big difference with electronic spreadsheets is that the columns and rows appear on a computer screen rather than on paper. Another difference is that spreadsheet calculations can be performed by the computer instead of manually. This tutorial is designed to explain exactly how Lotus 1-2-3 works.

If you are not already familiar with using a microcomputer, turn to Appendix A in this workbook before beginning Lesson 1. This appendix contains brief instructions on running the IBM PC, and on the care and handling of disks.

LESSON 1
BASIC DATA ENTRY

LOADING LOTUS 1-2-3 INTO THE COMPUTER

Before beginning this lesson, you should have the Lotus 1-2-3 System Disk and an IBM PC DOS or MS DOS disk (2.0 or higher). Insert the DOS disk into disk drive A and turn on the computer. The red light on the drive will go on and then will go out again. If requested by your computer, enter the date and then the time, pressing ENTER (⏎) after each entry. In a few more seconds, you will see the operating system prompt. This manual uses A> to represent the operating system prompt, but your prompt may look different. Remove the DOS disk and insert the Lotus 1-2-3 System Disk in drive A. Type **LOTUS** and press ENTER. (You may use either capital or lowercase letters. The commands that you are to enter from the keyboard are indicated in bold type.) Shortly, you will see the first Lotus screen. The heading will indicate that this is the Lotus Access System.

The Mode Indicator in the upper right corner of the screen contains the word MENU, and on the line below the heading you will see several words such as 1-2-3, PrintGraph, Translate, and so forth. Each of these represents an activity category that can be accessed by the Lotus program. The only one you will be concerned with now is 1-2-3. Press ENTER now and 1-2-3 will be loaded. With Version 1A, you will need to press one more key before the program will be ready to run. The computer monitor will appear as shown on the next page in Illustration 1.

If the program does not load properly, check to make sure that you have inserted the Lotus 1-2-3 System Disk and not another disk into the drive. After checking this, repeat the procedure described above. If you still have difficulty getting the program to load properly, contact your instructor.

Illustration 1
Lotus 1-2-3 Screen Display

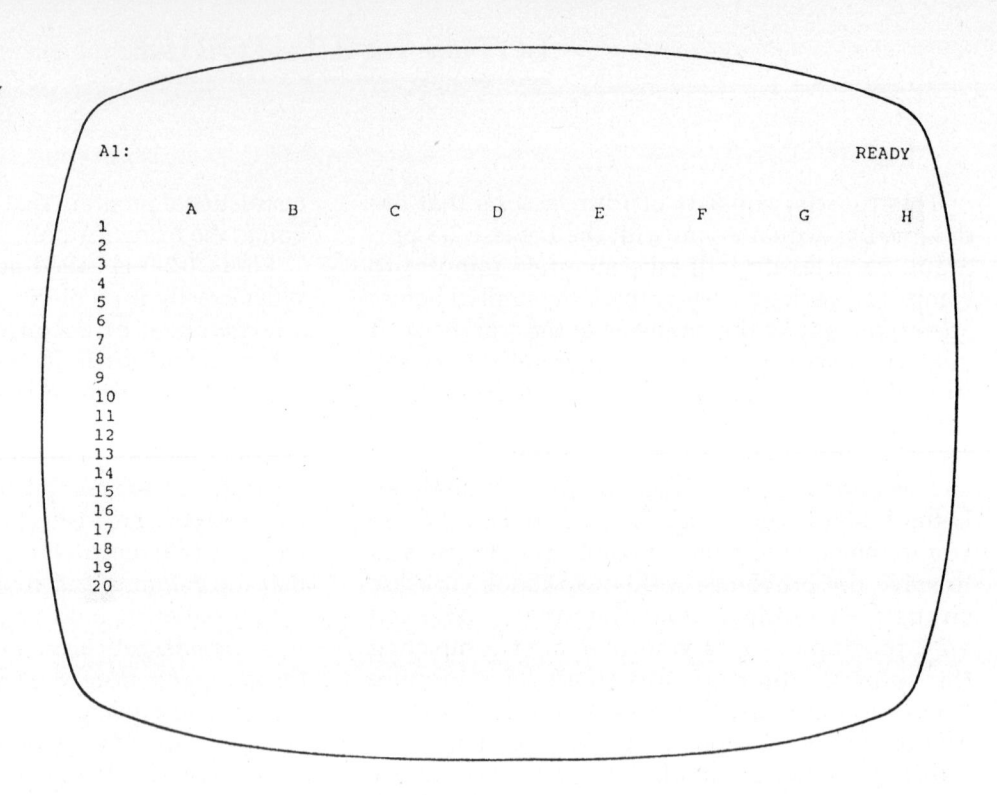

```
A1:                                                              READY

     A        B        C        D        E        F        G        H
 1
 2
 3
 4
 5
 6
 7
 8
 9
10
11
12
13
14
15
16
17
18
19
20
```

After the program is loaded, leave the 1-2-3 System Disk in the drive. There are occasions when it may be needed while you are working with the program.

USING THE ESCAPE (ESC) KEY

As you work through this tutorial, you will frequently be asked to enter commands to the computer using various keys on the keyboard. Occasionally, you may make a mistake by pressing the wrong key. When this occurs, you can use the ESCAPE (ESC) key to "escape" from the incorrect entry. Pressing the ESC key once or twice will eliminate the error and get you back to the READY mode (see the upper right corner of the screen). This will allow you to start over with the proper entry.

CURSOR MOVEMENT—ARROW KEYS

Notice that the screen is mostly blank but that there is a row of numbers down the side and letters in sequence (A, B, C, etc.) across the top. These numbers and letters frame the worksheet section of the program.

ARROW keys are on the right side of the keyboard under the numbers 2, 4, 6, and 8. Now, while watching the screen, press the RIGHT ARROW key on the keyboard. If you hear a short buzz, the program is telling you that you don't know your right from your left!

When the RIGHT ARROW key is depressed once, the highlighted rectangular box shifts over to a position under the B column. This box is known as the cursor (sometimes referred to as the cell pointer).

The area above the worksheet is called the Control Panel. Notice that there is a B1 in the upper left corner of the Control Panel. This indicates the position of the cursor on the worksheet. The letter "B" indicates the column and the number "1" indicates the row. Now use the LEFT ARROW key to move the cursor back to cell A1 and notice that the symbol in the Control Panel changes back to A1. The cursor indicates the position of the "active cell."

Now for one of the surprises of this program. Press the RIGHT ARROW key repeatedly until the cursor moves past the last column shown on the right side of the screen. Note that new columns appear in alphabetic sequence. This is called scrolling. You can speed up the cursor movement by depressing the RIGHT ARROW key and holding it down. If the computer starts to beep at you, take your finger off the RIGHT ARROW key momentarily to allow the cursor to catch up. The far right column is "IV." That's 256 columns!

1-2-3 also has more rows than are shown on the screen. Scroll the cursor downward and notice the row numbers change as you move the cursor past the last row shown on the screen. Stop when you get to row 100. It would take a long time for you to find the bottom of the worksheet since it is 8,192 rows deep! (Version 1A has 2048 rows and the Student Edition contains 64 columns and 256 rows.)

As you can see, the worksheet is very large. There are over two million cells that can be accessed. (Version 1A is limited to about half a million cells.) What shows on the screen is only a small portion of the entire area. The computer screen can be thought of as a window for viewing a small portion of the entire worksheet.

OTHER METHODS OF CURSOR MOVEMENT

There are several ways to move the cursor around the worksheet quickly that are particularly helpful for long distances. One method is to use the function key marked F5 on the left side of the keyboard. Press that key now. Remember, if you enter something incorrectly, use the ESC key. Notice the following message in the Control Panel:

Enter address to go to: xxxx

Ignore the cell reference (xxxx) for now. You are being asked to enter the particular location that you wish to move to. Type **A1** (either capital or lowercase letters may be used) and press the ENTER key. Bingo! The cursor will immediately move to cell A1.

Another way to move the cursor is to use the keys marked PG UP and PG DN. Press the PG DN key and watch what happens. This command moves the screen down 20 lines on the worksheet (a page). The PG UP key moves the screen up 20 lines. The TAB (↔) key does the same thing, moving the screen left and right. Use the SHIFT key with the TAB key to move the screen to the left. Go ahead and experiment with these four keys.

A third way to move long distances quickly is to use the END key. Regardless of where the cursor is now, press the END key once and then the RIGHT ARROW key once. What happens? As you can see, the END key/ARROW key combination moves the cursor to the END of the row or column that the cursor is on. (It will stop if it bumps into a cell that isn't empty.) Practice using the END key a while. See if you can get the cursor positioned in the lower right corner of the worksheet.

There is a fourth method that should also be mentioned here. Press the HOME key and watch what happens. The HOME key always moves the cursor to cell A1. This is a rather limited, but very helpful, key.

DATA ENTRY AND EDITING

You are ready to begin learning how to enter data on the spreadsheet and how to edit cell contents. There are two categories of data that may be entered on a spreadsheet: labels and values. The editing features of a spreadsheet allow you to make corrections and changes to these data.

Labels and Values

Labels are letters or words that are placed on a spreadsheet. With the cursor positioned in cell A1, type the word **COMPUTER**. Remember to use the ESC key if you make an error. You may use either capital or lowercase letters. Note that as soon as you type the letter C, the word LABEL appears in the Mode Indicator on the right side of the Control Panel.

Input is not actually stored in the cell until the ENTER key (or one of the ARROW keys) is pushed. Pressing one of the ARROW keys serves the dual purpose of storing input in a cell and moving the cursor in the direction of the arrow. This is particularly helpful when entering a large amount of data in a row or column. Press the ENTER key or one of the ARROW keys now. This action stores the label COMPUTER in cell A1.

Now position the cursor in cell A5, type your full name, and press ENTER. What happens? You will undoubtedly find that your name does not all fit in one cell. In fact, each cell holds only nine characters. If your label is longer than nine characters, it bleeds over to the next cell (as long as that cell is empty).

Move the cursor to cell G1, type the word **DOG**, and press ENTER. Now move the cursor to cell F1, type the words **PERSONAL COMPUTER**, and press ENTER. From the result, you can see that you must be careful when entering labels that bleed over to other cells.

Values are cell inputs that are either numbers or formulas. On the IBM PC, you may use either the number keys across the top of the keyboard or those on the keypad on the right side of the keyboard. To use the numbers on the keypad, press the NUM LOCK key once. This turns the numbers "on." To get the ARROW keys again, press the NUM LOCK key once more to turn the numbers "off." For this tutorial, do not use the number keys from the keypad since you need to use these keys as ARROW keys.

Lotus 1-2-3 Tutorial   151

Move the cursor to cell D11. Type the number **123** using the number keys across the top of the keyboard. As soon as the 1 is typed, note that the word VALUE appears in the Mode Indicator. Now press ENTER. The value 123 is now stored in cell D11.

The 1-2-3 program identifies your cell input as either a label or a value by the first character you enter in the cell. If it is a letter, the word LABEL appears in the Mode Indicator. If it is a number, the word VALUE appears.

Now that you are familiar with entering values, let's try a simple exercise. In cell A6 (right under your name) enter your home street address (for example: 27495 Short Street) and press ENTER. What happens? The program does not let you enter your address in the cell. In fact, as you can see by the Mode Indicator, you are now in the EDIT mode. The lesson here is that you cannot mix values and labels in the same cell. However, it is possible to enter numbers in a cell as a part of a label. To demonstrate this, you first have to get out of the EDIT mode. Press the ESC key twice to eliminate your address and get you out of the EDIT mode.

Now let's start over. With the cursor in cell A6, press the APOSTROPHE (') key. It is right under the QUOTATION MARK (") on the same key. Be careful; don't use the ACCENT (`) key right next door. The apostrophe triggers the 1-2-3 program to expect a label, as the Mode Indicator now shows. Now type your address and press ENTER. Your address should appear beginning in cell A6. The apostrophe should not show in the cell. You will need to use this technique every time you wish to enter a label in which the first character is a number.

Editing Cell Contents

If you make a typing error that you catch before you press the ENTER key, you may make a correction immediately by using the BACKSPACE (←) key. Each time you press the BACKSPACE key, a letter or digit is deleted. Move the cursor to cell B1, type **COMPTER** (but do not press ENTER), and then use the BACKSPACE key to eliminate the three incorrect letters (TER) and type the correct ones **(UTER)**. Press ENTER or one of the ARROW keys when the word has been corrected.

The ESC key may also be used to correct an error you catch before pressing ENTER. Pressing the ESC key will delete the whole entry. Move the cursor to cell C1, type the number **456**, but don't press ENTER. Now press the ESC key and watch the whole number be deleted.

If you make a typing error that you catch after you press ENTER, you may make a correction

using the key marked F2. To demonstrate this, move the cursor to cell C3, type the word **MACRO**, and press ENTER. Now let's change this word to MICRO. Press the F2 key. Use the LEFT ARROW key to position the blinking edit cursor under the letter to be deleted (the A in this case). Next press the DEL key to delete the letter A. Then type the correct letter (an **I**) and press ENTER.

If you wish to rewrite a cell's contents totally, simply position the cursor in that cell, type over what is already in the cell, and press ENTER. Let's try that now by changing the entry in cell A1 from COMPUTER to LOTUS. Move the cursor to cell A1, type the word **LOTUS**, and press ENTER. This is a quick way to change short labels or values.

If you wish to blank out a cell totally, you may simply use the SPACE BAR and the ENTER key. To demonstrate this, move the cursor to cell D11 (where you have entered 123), press the SPACE BAR and then the ENTER key. The contents of the cell will be erased. (Also, see the **Range Erase** command in Lesson 3.)

Move the cursor to cell G3, type the words **PERSONAL COMPUTER**, and press ENTER. Suppose you now wish to erase the word COMPUTER. Even though it appears that you should move to cell H3 to erase that word, that won't work because the word COMPUTER is really in cell G3. It bleeds into cell H3 when shown on the screen, but it is actually entered in cell G3. With the cursor still in cell G3, press the edit key (F2) and then the BACKSPACE key several times to eliminate the word COMPUTER. Press ENTER when done.

Arithmetic Calculations

The basic mathematical operations that 1-2-3 can perform are addition, subtraction, multiplication, division, and exponentiation. There are more complex mathematical functions that 1-2-3 can perform. Many of these are discussed in Lesson 4.

The table on the top of page 153 indicates the keyboard keys for each mathematical operation.

You will find all of the operator keys on the keyboard, some in more than one place. Let's try the addition example now. Remember to use the BACKSPACE and ESC keys to correct errors. Move the cursor to cell D12, type **123+456** and press ENTER. Immediately in the cell you will see the answer 579. Use cell D12 to try the other examples shown in the following table and check your answers. Remember to press ENTER after typing each example.

It is also possible to perform several mathematical operations at once. For example, the following is a perfectly acceptable formula to enter in a cell:

Operator Key	Description	Example	Explanation	Answer
+Plus Sign	Addition	123+456	Adds 123 and 456	579
-Dash	Subtraction	123-81	Subtracts 81 from 123	42
*Asterisk	Multiplication	123*1.2	Multiplies 123 by 1.2	147.6
/Slash	Division	123/7	Divides 123 by 7	17.571
^Caret	Exponentiation	123^2	Squares 123	15129

4+6/2-1. Enter this in cell D12 and see what happens. If you enter it correctly, the result will be 6.

The sequence in which the 1-2-3 program performs computations is as follows:

First: Exponentiation
Second: Multiplication and Division
Third: Addition and Subtraction

Just like high school algebra! Within each level of precedence, the calculations are performed from left to right. In the example above, the first operation performed is 6 divided by 2. Next, starting from the left, 4 is added to 3 and then 1 is subtracted for a result of 6.

If you wish to perform the computations in some other sequence, what can you do? Rearranging the formula is not always the answer. You can control the sequence of computations in 1-2-3 by using parentheses. The 1-2-3 program will always perform calculations inside a set of parentheses before doing any other arithmetic operations. Suppose in the preceding example that you want to add 4 and 6 and then divide by 2. Using parentheses, the formula would look as follows: **(4+6)/2-1**. Try it and see if you get 4 as the answer.

It is also possible to have several sets of parentheses in a single formula. For example: **9+(9*2)/(7-4)**. 1-2-3 will perform the operations inside both pairs of parentheses first (left set first), then do the division, and lastly do the addition. Enter this formula now. Your answer should be 15.

Parentheses may also be "nested" as shown in this example: **(9+(9*2))/3**. 1-2-3 will perform the operations in the innermost set of parentheses first and then will work outward to the next set. In this example, the program will multiply 9 by 2, add 9 to the result, and then divide by 3. The answer will be 9.

Without the parentheses the result would be quite different. Working in the natural order of precedence, 1-2-3 would multiply 9 by 2, divide the result by 3, and add 9 for an answer of 15.

Parentheses are used fairly frequently in 1-2-3 programming to direct the computer to the proper sequence of computations. The one thing you must remember is that there must always be an equal number of left and right parentheses in a formula. The formula (123/7*(-1.2*81) is incorrect because there are two left parentheses and only one right parenthesis.

1-2-3 COMMANDS

The 1-2-3 program contains commands that help manipulate the spreadsheet. These commands can only be entered when the program is in the READY mode. Press ESC (repeatedly, if necessary) until the Mode Indicator says READY. Then press the SLASH (/) key. A menu appears at the top of the screen in the Control Panel. The upper line of the menu appears at the bottom of this page.

In Version 2 and higher, the word System also appears. In addition, Version 2.2 shows Add-In. Each word in the sequence stands for a different command, as the table below indicates:

Worksheet	General commands affecting the whole worksheet
Range	Commands affecting specific portions of the worksheet
Copy	Copy a cell or range of cells
Move	Move a cell or range of cells
File	Commands affecting files saved on a storage disk
Print	Print a worksheet
Graph	Graphical display of worksheet data
Data	Special data manipulation commands
System	Exit to DOS (not available in Version 1A)
Add-In	Allows access to programs written by developers (Version 2.2)
Quit	End 1-2-3 session; exit to Lotus Access System Menu

Worksheet   Range   Copy   Move   File   Print   Graph   Data   Quit

All of the 1-2-3 commands that are pertinent to the problems in the workbook will be introduced in this tutorial. Press ESC now to clear the menu.

HELP Key (F1)

1-2-3 uses the function key marked F1 as a HELP key. Any time you have questions on the particular command you are entering, press the F1 key. Immediately the screen will fill with instructions and information. Use the ARROW keys to maneuver around the HELP screen. Press ESC to get back to the worksheet. Try the F1 key now if you wish. With Version 2.2, the Help program has been placed on a separate Help Disk which you must insert in drive A before the F1 key is pressed. Press ESC to get back to the worksheet when done. (Warning: If you are using someone else's copy of Lotus 1-2-3, do not be surprised if the HELP key (F1) doesn't work. The owners of the Lotus 1-2-3 disks frequently delete the Help program from the Lotus 1-2-3 System Disk to create more room to store other programs.)

READY Mode

As mentioned previously, 1-2-3 commands can only be executed with the program in the READY mode. It is easy to forget this. To demonstrate a common error, move the cursor to cell B17, type **PLAY**, and do not press ENTER. Suppose you now decide to enter a command from the menu shown above. Press the SLASH (/) key. Why doesn't the menu appear in the Control Panel? The menu does not appear because the program accepted the slash key as a label rather than as a command (note that the Mode Indicator says LABEL). Press ENTER now to store PLAY/ in B17. Now the program will be in the READY mode and will accept commands.

Using the Undo Feature (Versions 2.2 and 3 only)

When you are in the READY Mode, Versions 2.2 and 3 allow you to reverse or cancel the last thing you did. For example, the last steps you performed were to erase PLAY/ from cell B17. Suppose you now decide you want PLAY/ in cell B17. To undo your erasure, hold down the ALT key and press the F4 key once. You notice now that PLAY/ reappears in cell B17. The undo feature is very helpful for recovering from mistakes. It can only be used to undo the last 1-2-3 command sequence entered.

Escape or Control Break

Spreadsheet commands can always be deleted by using the ESC key. However, ESC will have to be pressed several times to escape fully a command that has several subcommands. A quicker way to delete completely a command that has already been entered is to press the CTRL key and the BREAK key simultaneously. The BREAK key (also labeled as SCROLL LOCK) is in the upper right corner of the keyboard. Pressing these two keys at the same time will immediately delete any commands currently entered.

CLEARING THE SCREEN

What you have on the screen now is a bunch of doodles. Let's clear the screen to get a fresh start and do something important! Erasing the worksheet requires a series of commands. Since this is the first time you have used the 1-2-3 commands, each step will be thoroughly explained.

Check to make sure you are in the READY mode. Press the SLASH (/) key to see the menu of commands. Notice that the word "Worksheet" in the menu is highlighted. This highlighted box is called the menu pointer. The LEFT and RIGHT ARROW keys are used to move the menu pointer to the desired command. Press the RIGHT ARROW key to move the menu pointer to the word "Range." Notice that the words on the line under the main menu change as you move the menu pointer. The second line shows the description or subcommands that apply to the highlighted command. Use the ARROW keys now to move the menu pointer across the top of the screen, and check the subcommands and descriptions shown for each command.

Now let's locate the specific command to erase the worksheet. As mentioned previously, the command category Worksheet contains commands that affect the worksheet as a whole. Since you want to erase the whole worksheet, you will begin with this command. Move the menu pointer to Worksheet

---

| Global | Insert | Delete | Column-Width | Erase | Titles | Window | Status |

and press ENTER to select this command. Remember to use the ESC key or the CTRL and BREAK keys if you make any erroneous keystrokes.

Once you have selected the command, you are presented with the menu of subcommands which appears at the bottom of the previous page. In Version 2 and higher, the word Column-Width has been shortened to Column, and the word Page has been added.

Now you must select the subcommand that will erase the worksheet. Press the RIGHT ARROW key four times to move the menu pointer to the word "Erase" and press ENTER to select this subcommand.

The next menu options are "No" or "Yes." Press the RIGHT ARROW key to position the menu pointer on Yes, press ENTER, and the screen is erased. Selecting No would stop the Erase command from being executed.

Let's review the steps needed to erase the worksheet:

Press the SLASH (/) key.
Press ENTER to select the Worksheet command.
Press the RIGHT ARROW key four times to move the menu pointer to Erase.
Press ENTER to select the Erase command.
Press the RIGHT ARROW key once to move the menu pointer to Yes.
Press ENTER to select Yes.

That's nine keystrokes to erase the worksheet. There is a shorter way. To demonstrate the shortcut, type the word **GOODBYE** in cell B2 and press ENTER. With the method used above, the RIGHT and LEFT ARROW keys are used to find the command desired and the ENTER key is used to select it. The quicker method is to select the commands by simply typing the first letter of the command options. To demonstrate this, execute the following instructions:

Press the SLASH (/) key.
Press **W** to select Worksheet.
Press **E** to select Erase.
Press **Y** to select Yes.

Only four keystrokes with this method! Either method can be used when entering commands, but you will generally find the "letter" technique quicker.

This completes Lesson 1. If you wish to stop here, key /QY. Choose Exit from the Lotus Access System Menu, and you're done. If you wish to continue, leave the computer on and begin Lesson 2.

LESSON 2

BASIC SPREADSHEET MODELING

Before you begin this lesson, the 1-2-3 program should be loaded and you should be staring at a blank worksheet. Refer to Lesson 1 if you need help loading the program. You should also have the Template Disk that is included with the workbook you purchased.

WORKSHEET SETUP AND FORMULAS

Let's set up a simple income statement. Enter the labels listed below. The cells where you are to put the labels are shown on the left, followed by a colon. The labels are shown on the right side of the colon. For example, A3: **SALES** means to put the label **SALES** in cell A3 and then press ENTER (or an ARROW key). You may use capital and/or lowercase letters. Remember to use the BACKSPACE key or the ESC key to correct errors. Note that several of these entries extend into column B.

> A3: **SALES**
> A5: **SELLING EXPENSES**
> A6: **GENERAL EXPENSES**
> A8: **TOTAL EXPENSES**
> A10: **NET INCOME**

Now let's enter some values into the statement. Enter the following amount for sales:

> C3:**100**

Next, assume that selling expenses are 60% of sales. You will enter a formula to compute selling expenses in cell C5. The formula will tell the program to take the value in cell C3, multiply it by .6, and put the result in cell C5. You have to use the plus sign (+) in front of the "C3" to indicate to the 1-2-3 program that C3 is to be treated as a value and not as a label. Enter the following formula for selling expenses:

> C5:**+C3*.6**

The 1-2-3 program will perform the calculation, and the result (60) will be entered in cell C5. THIS FORMULA METHOD IS THE MOST IMPORTANT FEATURE OF THE 1-2-3 PROGRAM. It is what makes spreadsheet programs so flexible and powerful. This point will become more apparent as you proceed through the tutorial.

Now enter the value for general expenses in cell C6 as follows:

> C6:**19**

In cell C8 you will enter the sum of the two expenses. You could simply enter the formula **+C5+C6.** However, there is another way to accom~plish the same thing. 1-2-3 has a summation function that allows you to add a row or column of figures quickly. To demonstrate this function, enter the following formula for total expenses:

> C8:**@SUM(C5.C6)**

Entering **@SUM** tells 1-2-3 to use the summation function. The first cell, C5, tells the computer where to begin the addition, and the last cell, C6, tells the computer the last cell to include in the total. This method is particularly useful for summing long rows or columns. You should note that when you enter the period (.), the computer responds with two periods (..). This is perfectly normal.

Now let's enter the last formula. Net income is computed by subtracting total expenses (C8) from sales (C3). Hence the formula will be as follows:

> C10:**+C3-C8**

After you have entered the above formula, you will have completed the simple income statement. It should appear as shown in Illustration 2, at the top of page 157.

Let's play with it a little. Notice that net income is $21. How much would it be if January sales were $110? Move the cursor back up to cell C3. Type in the number 110 (just type it right over 100) and press ENTER. What happens? The income statement is automatically updated as the input changes. Try 120. Try 200. This is often referred to as playing what-if. Now you are beginning to witness what an electronic spreadsheet is all about!

LABEL ALIGNMENT

To begin exploring spreadsheet commands in detail, let's expand the income statement developed above from one month to six months. So we all begin with the same numbers, reset the value in cell C3 to **100**.

Now move the cursor to cell C1, enter the letters **JAN** (short for January), and press ENTER. JAN now appears in cell C1, but it is not aligned above the numbers. This is because values are aligned to the right side of cells and labels are aligned to the left. Label alignment can be changed in one of three ways: a single cell can be realigned; all labels on the

Illustration 2
Income Statement

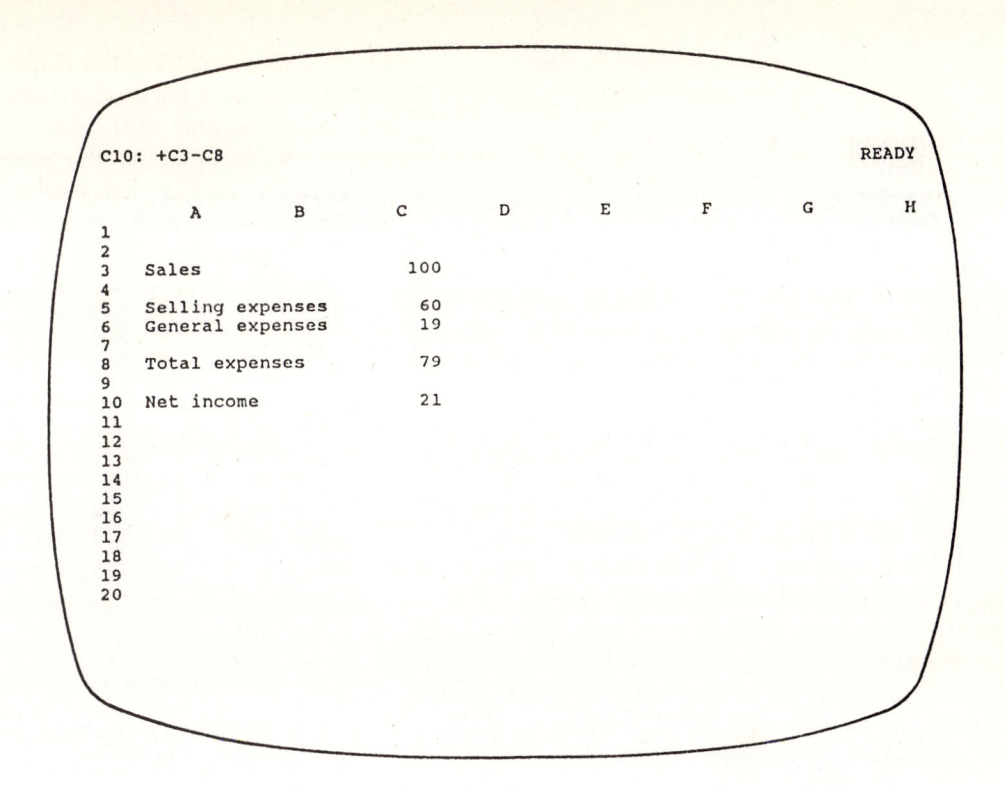

```
C10: +C3-C8                                                    READY

         A         B         C         D         E         F         G         H
 1
 2
 3   Sales                   100
 4
 5   Selling expenses         60
 6   General expenses         19
 7
 8   Total expenses           79
 9
10   Net income               21
11
12
13
14
15
16
17
18
19
20
```

worksheet can be realigned; or a specific range of labels can be realigned. The procedures for each of these options will be discussed below.

Aligning a Label in a Single Cell

The label in a single cell can be realigned by putting a code character in front of the label. Type each of the following examples in cell C1 and watch what happens (press ENTER after each example):

Code Character	Example	Result
Quotation mark	"JAN	Right aligned
Apostrophe	'JAN	Left aligned
Caret	^JAN	Centered
Backslash	\JAN	Repeating

Before we discuss the other options for label alignment, enter "JAN in cell C1 to position the heading over the values in column C.

Aligning All Labels on the Worksheet

One command will affect the alignment of all labels on the worksheet. Enter the following command now: **/WGLR** (Worksheet Global Label-Prefix **Right**).

You have just told the computer to align all labels to the right side of cells. This does not affect labels already entered. Note, for example, that the position of the word SALES is unaffected by this command. To see what this command does, let's add headings for each month by entering the following:

D1: **FEB**
E1: **MAR**
F1: **APR**
G1: **MAY**
H1: **JUN**
I1: **TOTAL**

Notice that after pressing ENTER, each of your entries is right aligned in its cell. The other alignment options available are:

For left alignment: **/WGLL** (Worksheet Global-Label-Prefix **L**eft)

For centered labels: **/WGLC** (Worksheet Global Label-Prefix **C**enter)

You can override these global alignment commands for individual cells by using the single-cell code characters shown in the previous section or by the Range Label-Prefix commands discussed next.

Aligning Labels in a Range

Using the Range command you can affect the alignment of labels on a portion of the worksheet. The labels in a range can be right aligned, left aligned, or centered. To realign the labels in row 1 using the Range command, position the cursor in cell C1 and enter **/RLL** (**R**ange **L**abel **L**eft). Above the worksheet you now see the following:

Lotus 1-2-3 Tutorial   157

Enter range of labels: C1..C1

You can respond in one of four ways: press ENTER to accept the computer's suggestion; use the ARROW keys to enter your own range (called "pointing"); type the beginning and ending cell references to specify the range; or press ESC to stop and back up or CTRL BREAK to stop the command completely. Each of these options may be used whenever the 1-2-3 program asks you to specify a range of cells. A discussion of the first three options, with an example of each, follows. The fourth option, to use the ESC or CTRL BREAK keys, was discussed in Lesson 1.

1. By pressing ENTER, you accept the program's suggested range, which is a single cell. Press ENTER now and you should find that JAN has been moved to the left side of the cell.
2. By using the ARROW keys you can point to your own range beginning with the current cursor position and ending with the cell to which the cursor is moved. To demonstrate the pointing technique, position the cursor in cell C1 and enter /RLL (Range Label Left) again. Now, in response to "Enter range of labels: C1..C1," press the RIGHT ARROW key once. Notice that the cursor moves to cell D1 and that the range is now C1..D1. Press the RIGHT ARROW key five more times. The range becomes C1..I1. Now, as an experiment, press the DOWN ARROW key five times. As you can see, this causes the range to expand into a box shape. Press ENTER and see what effect the alignment command has on the labels and values. From the result, you can see that alignment commands only affect labels.
3. You may also specify your own range by typing the beginning and ending cell references. For example, move the cursor to cell I8 and enter /RLR (Range Label Right). Now type **C1.I1** and press ENTER. The labels in the range from C1 to I1 are now right aligned. The advantage of this method is that the cursor can be positioned anywhere on the worksheet at the time you enter the command.

COPY (/C)

The Copy command allows you to take the contents of one cell and copy it into another cell. It also allows you to copy the contents of a range of cells (source range) into another range of cells (target range). This is an extremely important and powerful command.

To demonstrate the Copy command, let's fill in the numbers for each month on your income statement. Assume that sales will increase by 2% per month. In other words, you want February's sales to be 2% greater than January's, March's sales to be 2% greater than February's, and so forth. To compute February's sales, you want to tell the computer to multiply January's sales, cell C3, by 1.02. The result will be entered in cell D3. Enter the following formula in cell D3:

D3:+C3*1.02

Since you want this 2% increase to be computed for each month, you can now use the Copy command to enter the correct formula in each of the remaining sales cells. With the cursor in cell D3, press the SLASH (/) key and then select the Copy command. In the Control Panel, you will see the following:

Enter range to copy FROM: D3..D3

The program is asking you to identify the source range. In this case, your source range is simply one cell, since you are only interested in copying the formula in cell D3. The computer already shows this cell (D3..D3) as the source range, so simply press ENTER now. If there were a range of cells to be copied, you would enter that range (by pointing or typing) before pressing ENTER. This will be demonstrated later.

Now that the source range has been entered, the program wants to know what the target range is. In other words, it wants to know TO which cells the contents of cell D3 are to be copied. Since the remaining sales figures are to appear in cells E3 through H3, enter **E3**, press the PERIOD (.) key, and enter **H3**. Press ENTER and watch what happens. Bingo! The formulas and the answers are put into cells E3 through H3 as shown in Illustration 3, at the top of page 159. The numbers are inconsistent in format, some having no decimal point and others having a decimal point followed by several digits, but you will take care of this problem later.

Notice the sequence of sales figures. Each month is a 2% increase over the previous month. The formula in cell D3 is +C3*1.02. Move the cursor to cell E3, and check the formula in that cell. You will see that the formula is +D3*1.02. Move the cursor to F3, G3, and H3 and look at the formulas. You will find that the formula in cell D3 was not copied exactly, but rather was modified as it moved from cell to cell.

The Copy command copies the formula from cell to cell and automatically modifies the formula to follow the same pattern as in the original formula. In this case, the original formula in cell D3 uses a

Illustration 3
Income Statement After Copying of Sales Cells

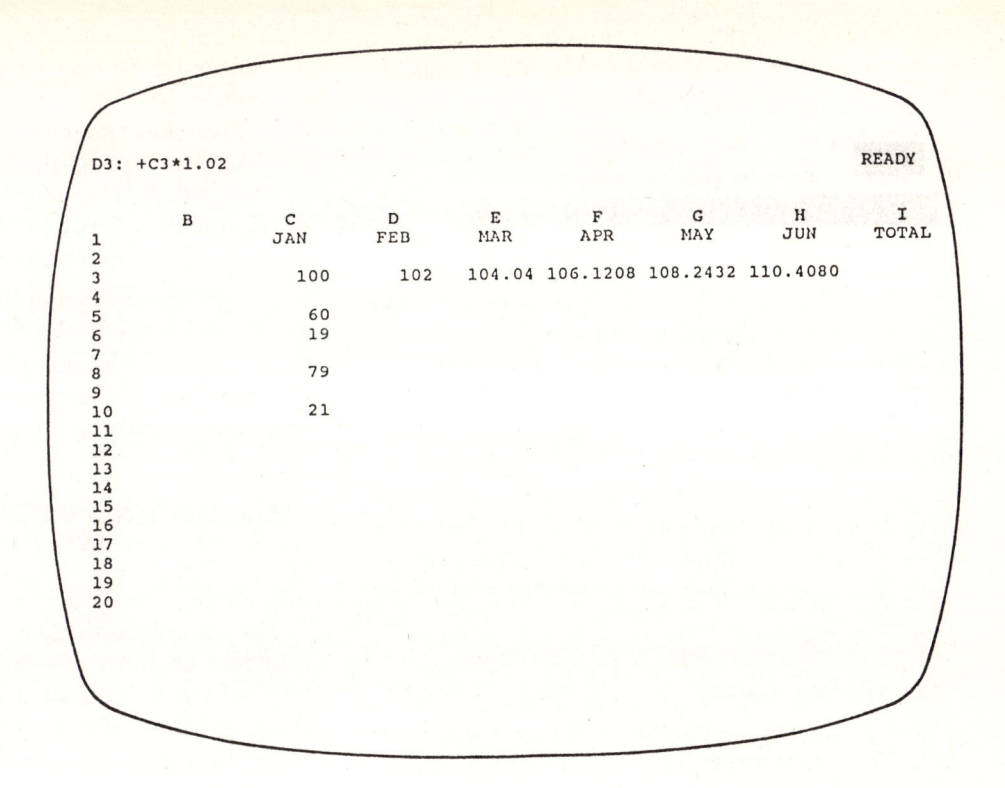

```
D3: +C3*1.02                                                    READY

           B        C       D       E        F        G        H        I
                   JAN     FEB     MAR      APR      MAY      JUN     TOTAL
 1
 2
 3                 100     102    104.04  106.1208 108.2432 110.4080
 4
 5                  60
 6                  19
 7
 8                  79
 9
10                  21
11
12
13
14
15
16
17
18
19
20
```

value from the cell to its immediate left (C3). Thus, when copying this formula, each new formula will also use a value from the cell to its immediate left. When copying formulas, the 1-2-3 program assumes that all cell references are "relative" and are to be modified from cell to cell.

What if you want to copy a formula but you do not want the cell references to change? There is a simple way to do this. By entering a dollar sign ($) in front of any cell reference used in a formula, you tell the computer that the cell reference is "absolute" (does not change). To compare the effects of absolute versus relative copying of formulas, examine the table shown at the bottom of this page.

To demonstrate the absolute copying option, perform the following steps:

1. Move the cursor to cell D3, retype the formula as **C3*1.02**, and press ENTER.
2. Enter **/C** to begin copying.
3. Press ENTER to complete the source range.
4. Type **E3.H3** and press ENTER to complete the target range.

You can see by the results that the cell reference C3 was not changed from cell to cell. Each month's sales are the same—a 2% increase over January's sales (C3).

Since you want each month's sales to be a 2% increase over each preceding month's, let's change it back to the way it was. This time, however, you will use the pointing technique.

1. In cell D3 enter the formula **+C3*1.02** and press ENTER.
2. Enter **/C** to begin copying.
3. Press the ENTER key to complete the source range.
4. Press the RIGHT ARROW key once. This selects cell E3 as the beginning cell in the target range.
5. Press the PERIOD (.) key to lock in your choice.
6. Press the RIGHT ARROW key three times to select H3 as the ending cell in the target range.
7. Press ENTER to complete the copying.

All of the above examples of copying involved a source range that was a single cell (D3). As mentioned previously, you can also use the Copy command to copy several formulas (a range) at once. To demonstrate this, let's copy each of the remaining

	C3 is Absolute	**C3 is Relative**
Original Formula	D3: C3*1.02	D3: C3*1.02
Copy	E3: C3*1.02	E3: C3*1.02
Copy	F3: C3*1.02	F3: C3*1.02
Copy	G3: C3*1.02	G3: C3*1.02

Lotus 1-2-3 Tutorial 159

January formulas and values to the other months. Perform the following steps:

1. Position the cursor in cell C5.
2. Enter **/C** to begin the copying.
3. Press the DOWN ARROW key five times to move the cursor to cell C10.
4. Press ENTER to complete the source range.
5. Press the RIGHT ARROW key once to move the cursor to the first cell in the target range (D5).
6. Press the PERIOD (.) key to lock in your choice.
7. Press the RIGHT ARROW key four times to move the cursor to the ending point in the target range (H5). Note that when the source range is more than one cell, the target range indicates only where the first cell in the source range is to be placed. Hence the target range is only a single row of cells and not a block of cells.
8 Press ENTER to complete the copying.

In a few short steps, you have entered income statement data for six months! It is now time to fill in the TOTAL column. Move the cursor to cell I3 and enter the following formula to compute total sales for the six-month period:

I3:@SUM(C3.H3)

Now you will copy this summation formula to rows 4 through 8 using the following steps:

1. Position the cursor in cell I3.
2. Enter **/C** to begin the copying.
3. Press ENTER to complete the source range.
4. Enter **I5.I10** and press ENTER for the target range.
5. Move the cursor to cell I7, key **/RE** for Range Erase and press the ENTER key. Do the same for cell I9. This step is necessary because the summation formula has been copied into these cells but is not needed there.

After copying, your income statement should appear as shown in Illustration 4. The income statement looks a little messy right now, but basically it is done! You will now learn some commands that will help you tidy up the statement's appearance.

FORMATTING VALUES ON THE ENTIRE WORKSHEET

Now it is time to clean up the appearance of the numbers on the worksheet. This is called formatting values. To format values on the entire worksheet, enter **/WGF** now. The Control Panel will display the menu of options available to you, as shown at the top of page 161 (Versions 2, 2.01, and 2.2 also include the command Hidden).

Press F to examine the Fixed option. You are asked the number of decimal places to be shown. The computer offers the choice of two decimal places. You may either accept two decimal places by pressing ENTER, or you may type the desired number of places and then press ENTER. Let's accept the computer's offer of two decimal places. Simply press ENTER and watch what happens!

Illustration 4
Completed Income Statement (Columns B Through I)

```
I9:                                                                    READY

       B        C        D        E        F        G        H        I
1               JAN      FEB      MAR      APR      MAY      JUN      TOTAL
2
3               100      102      104.04   106.1208 108.2432 110.4080 630.8120
4
5               60       61.2     62.424   63.67248 64.94592 66.24484 378.4872
6               19       19       19       19       19       19       114
7
8               79       80.2     81.424   82.67248 83.94592 85.24484 492.4872
9
10              21       21.8     22.616   23.44832 24.29728 25.16323 138.3248
11
12
13
14
15
16
17
18
19
20
```

160 Lotus 1-2-3 Tutorial

```
          Fixed    Scientific    Currency   ,   General   +/-   Percent   Date   Text
```

Instantly, all values are displayed with two decimal places.

Now let's try the same thing with zero decimal places. Enter **/WGFF** to select the Fixed option. Now type in **0** (zero) and press ENTER. The screen now shows all integers.

Take a minute now and try the other formats listed below. These are the formats most frequently used in 1-2-3. Enter **/WGF** and then either use the ARROW keys to move the menu pointer to the format of your choice, or enter the first letter of your choice. The following table lists each format and its result:

Format	Result
Fixed	Fixed number of decimal places (0-15). No commas used.
Currency	Numbers expressed as dollars and cents. Dollar sign before each entry. Commas between thousands. Negative numbers in parentheses.
, (comma)	Same as the Currency format without the dollar signs.
General	Initial display format shown.
Percent	All numbers expressed as percents.
Text	Shows the formulas in each cell.
Hidden	Hides all entries on the worksheet (Versions 2, 2.01, and 2.2 only).

After you have experimented with these formats, please reset the worksheet to the General format (**/WGFG**).

FORMATTING A RANGE OF VALUES

The above commands apply to the worksheet as a whole. Values can also be formatted using the Range command, which affects a smaller grouping of cells. To demonstrate this, move the cursor to cell C3 and type **/RF**. You will now see the same list of options that were available under the Worksheet command. Let's put row 3 (Sales) and row 10 (Net Income) in the Currency format. Press **C** (for Currency) and then press ENTER to accept the computer's offer of two decimal places. Type the range **C3.I3** and press ENTER again. Then, with the cursor still in cell C3, enter the same series of commands (**/RFC**), except enter the range as **C10.I10**.

Next, use the following steps to format the remaining cells using the **,** (comma) format and the pointing technique.

1. Move the cursor to cell C5.
2. Enter **/RF,** (be sure you type the comma!).
3. Press ENTER to accept two decimal places.
4. Press the PERIOD key to lock in C5 as the beginning of the range.
5. Press the RIGHT ARROW key six times to move the cursor to column I. Then press the DOWN ARROW key three times to move to row 8 to complete the format range.
6. Press ENTER.

Notice that the statement format is much more organized and attractive when you're done.

UNDERLINES AND BORDERS

To improve appearance and readability, let's now add underlines, double underlines, and borders in appropriate locations in our model. Move the cursor to cell C2 where we will begin underlining the month headings. Underlines for headings should be at least as long as the headings themselves and should have at least one blank space between the columns. Each cell generally holds nine characters, and these are no exception. Let's go with underlines that are seven characters long and are centered in each cell. In cell C2, press the Space Bar, then type seven dashes (Minus Signs), and press ENTER.

Now copy this to other cells in row 2:

1. Enter **/C** and press ENTER.
2. Press the Right Arrow key once.
3. Press the Period key.
4. Press the Right Arrow key five more times.
5. Press ENTER.

The underlines also need to be placed in row 7. Use the following steps to copy the row of dashes in row 2 to row 7:

1. With the cursor in cell C2, press **/C**.
2. To indicate the source range, type C2.I2 and press ENTER.
3. Move the cursor to cell C7 and press ENTER.

Use the same three steps above to copy the underlines to row 9. (In Step 3, move the cursor to cell C9, rather than cell C7.)

In cell C11, we will put a double underline. Move the cursor to cell C11 and press the Space Bar, then type seven Equal Signs (=), and press ENTER. Use the Copy command to copy the Equal Signs to cells D11 through I11. If you need assistance, refer to the five steps above.

Illustration 5
Completed Income Statement
with Border
(Columns A Through H)

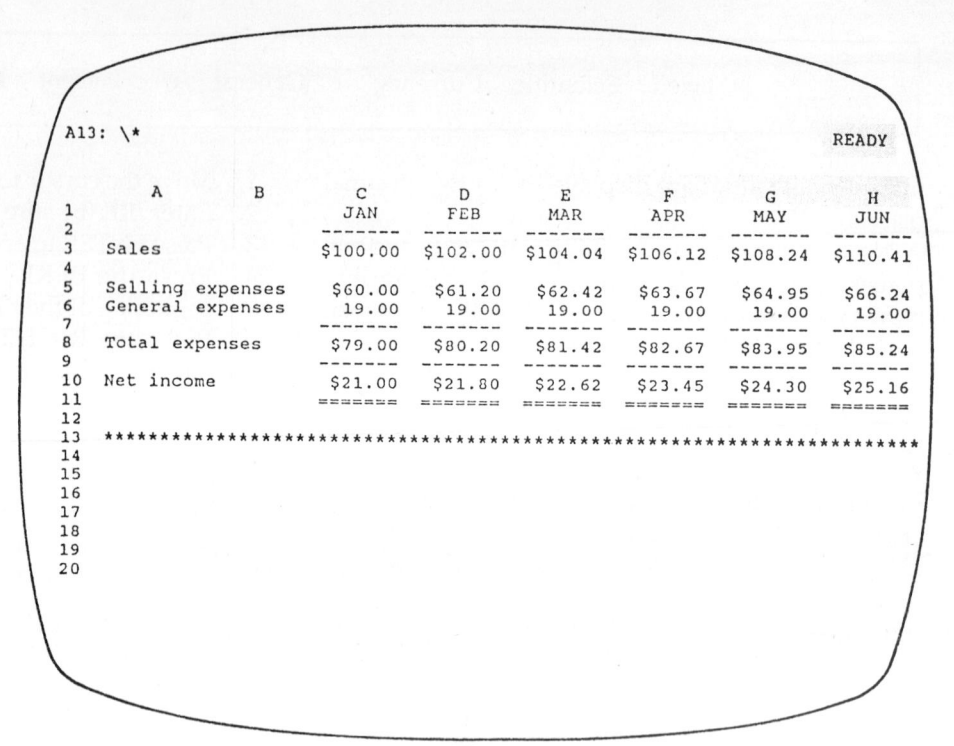

```
A13: \*                                                              READY

            A         B       C        D        E        F        G        H
 1                           JAN      FEB      MAR      APR      MAY      JUN
 2                         -------  -------  -------  -------  -------  -------
 3        Sales           $100.00  $102.00  $104.04  $106.12  $108.24  $110.41
 4
 5        Selling expenses $60.00   $61.20   $62.42   $63.67   $64.95   $66.24
 6        General expenses  19.00    19.00    19.00    19.00    19.00    19.00
 7                         -------  -------  -------  -------  -------  -------
 8        Total expenses   $79.00   $80.20   $81.42   $82.67   $83.95   $85.24
 9                         -------  -------  -------  -------  -------  -------
10        Net income       $21.00   $21.80   $22.62   $23.45   $24.30   $25.16
11                         =======  =======  =======  =======  =======  =======
12
13        ****************************************************************
14
15
16
17
18
19
20
```

As you may recall, the BACKSLASH (\) key is the code character for repeating labels. Let's add a border to the income statement by using the BACKSLASH (\) key. Move the cursor to cell I13. Type the BACKSLASH (\) key, then the ASTERISK (*) key, and press ENTER. Cell I13 should now be filled with asterisks.

Let's take this one step further and copy cell I13 to cells A13 through H13. With the cursor in cell I13, type /C and press ENTER to complete the source range. Then type **A13.I13** to complete the target range. Press ENTER and watch what happens! These steps put a border at the bottom of your income statement. Your completed income statement should appear as shown in Illustration 5, at the top of this page.

PERFORMING WHAT-IF ANALYSIS

The income statement model is now completed. You can ask what-if questions with this model by moving the cursor to cell C3 and entering different values. Enter **110** in cell C3 and press ENTER. Notice that the net income is instantly recalculated for all six months! Feel free to try out other numbers in cell C3.

NUMERICAL INPUT ERRORS

Certain entries in cell C3 will cause strange results. For example, enter the number **150** in cell C3. Notice that May's net income appears to be off by a penny. This is because 1-2-3 rounds off each cell to the nearest penny for screen presentation but it internally stores the value of each cell up to fifteen decimal places. Internally, it is computing net income correctly, but when it rounds off each cell to present the result, occasionally a rounding difference will occur. This can happen in other formats, too. There is a special function command discussed in Lesson 4 that will correct this problem.

Enter **10,000** in cell C3 and press ENTER. From the result, you can see that numbers are not to be entered with commas! Press ESC to get back to the READY mode.

Now type **100000** (one hundred thousand) and press ENTER. What happens? The number doesn't show up in the cell, does it? It is too large for the cell and the result you see is the way 1-2-3 tells you this.

Now type the word **HELLO** in cell C3 and press ENTER. Under Versions 1A, 2.01, and 2.2, the reason that zeros appear in many cells is that the 1-2-3 program assigns the numerical value of zero to all labels. Since cell C3 is now a label, it is given the value of zero and this subsequently affects many other cells. Under Version 2, labels are not given a numerical value. Therefore, any cell with a value dependent on C3 will show ERR.

Now, reset the value in cell C3 to **100**. The examples above demonstrate typical input errors. Keep them in mind when entering numerical data.

FILE COMMANDS (/F)

You are going to electronically transfer the income statement from the computer's memory (where it currently resides) to a permanent storage area. This will allow you to reuse the statement any time you want to without having to retype it. Move the cursor to cell A1 before storing.

The permanent storage area is the Template Disk provided with this workbook. Insert the Template Disk in drive B. Now press the SLASH (/) key and then type F (for File). The subcommands for the File command will appear as shown at the bottom of this page.

The subcommand Save is what you want. Press S now for Save. The program will respond with the following:

Enter save file name:

This is 1-2-3's way of asking you for a name for your file. (With Versions 2, 2.01, and 2.2, you will see "Enter save file name: B:".) On the line below this there are several strange words. These are the names of the files that are already on your disk. Each name represents a separate preprogrammed file that corresponds to a problem in the workbook. You will have a chance to look at these later. For now, just type the name SAMPLE and press the ENTER key. (File names cannot be longer than eight letters or numbers; either capital or lowercase letters are acceptable; no punctuation or spaces allowed.) The disk drive will jump to life and then after a few seconds will stop. You have now saved your income statement as a file called SAMPLE. In Versions 2, 2.01, and 2.2, 1-2-3 will add .WK1 to the end of your file name.

If there were already a file on the disk named SAMPLE, the program would ask you one further question:

Cancel   Replace   Backup (Versions 2.2 and 3 only)

You cannot have two files with the same name on the storage disk. If you press R, the old file will be replaced with the new one. If you don't want to replace the old file, you would press C and then choose another name for the new file.

With the Template Disk still in the drive, use the Worksheet Erase command to clear the worksheet from the screen (/WEY). Don't worry, this command will not erase the file from the disk. It erases only from the screen.

After using the Worksheet Erase command you should be looking at a blank worksheet. Let's bring the income statement back on the screen now. Enter /F to get the File subcommands again and then press R to select the Retrieve subcommand. The 1-2-3 program responds as follows:

Enter name of file to retrieve:

Type the name SAMPLE and press ENTER. The disk drive should start up and the income statement will soon appear on the screen. The cursor will appear in exactly the same spot it was left when the file was saved. There is another way to enter file names using the ARROW keys. This will be discussed in Lesson 3.

Although the file SAMPLE is now on the screen, it is also still recorded on the disk. It has simply been "read" into the computer. It will stay on the disk and can be used over and over until you actually erase it. (To erase a file from the disk, enter /FEW [File Erase Worksheet] and then type the name of the file to be erased.)

The other File subcommands are very powerful and helpful, but are beyond the scope of this tutorial.

This lesson is now finished! You are certainly welcome to go on immediately to Lesson 3. If you wish to stop now, refer to page 155 for instructions.

Retrieve   Save   Combine   Xtract   Erase   List   Import   Directory

Lotus 1-2-3 Tutorial

LESSON 3

ADDITIONAL SPREADSHEET COMMANDS

The goal of this lesson is to introduce most of the remaining 1-2-3 commands that are activated by the SLASH (/) key. In this lesson, you will be dealing with the file named SAMPLE, which you created and saved in Lesson 2. If that file is not currently loaded into the computer, please load it now from your Template Disk. Recall that the 1-2-3 program must be loaded before you can load a file. Refer to the File Retrieve command in Lesson 2 if you do not remember how to load a file. The file SAMPLE should appear as shown in Illustration 6.

Although you will be experimenting with commands that alter the worksheet shown above, it should be noted that your manipulations will not affect the saved version of SAMPLE on the Template Disk. The alterations that you make to the income statement model change the worksheet only as it appears on the screen. In order to change the version of SAMPLE on the disk, you would have to use the File command to save your revisions formally.

Relax and enjoy this lesson! The hard part is over. By the end of this lesson, you will be very aware that there is a lot to Lotus 1-2-3 that you still do not know, but you should feel fairly comfortable using Lotus and exploring new features of the Lotus program.

WORKSHEET COMMANDS

As discussed in Lesson 2, **Worksheet** commands are general commands that affect the entire spreadsheet. Two of the Worksheet Global subcommands (Format[/**WGF**] and Label-prefix [/**WGL**]), as well as the Worksheet Erase (/**WE**) command, have already been discussed. Several of the other Worksheet Global subcommands and the rest of the Worksheet commands (except Worksheet Page for Version 2 and Version 2.01) will now be discussed.

Global Column-Width (/WGC)

The standard column width (9 characters) may be changed to any number of characters between 1 and 240. You may want wide cells to be able to enter large numbers, or narrow cells to fit more columns on the screen. This command is global. It affects all columns. The column width for a single column can be adjusted using the **Column-Width** command (/**WC**). This will be discussed later.

To change the column width of all columns, enter /**WGC** now. You will be asked to enter a column width; enter **8** and press ENTER. Bingo! All the columns are shortened by one space. This allows both column A and column I to be seen on

Illustration 6
Income Statement
Saved as File SAMPLE

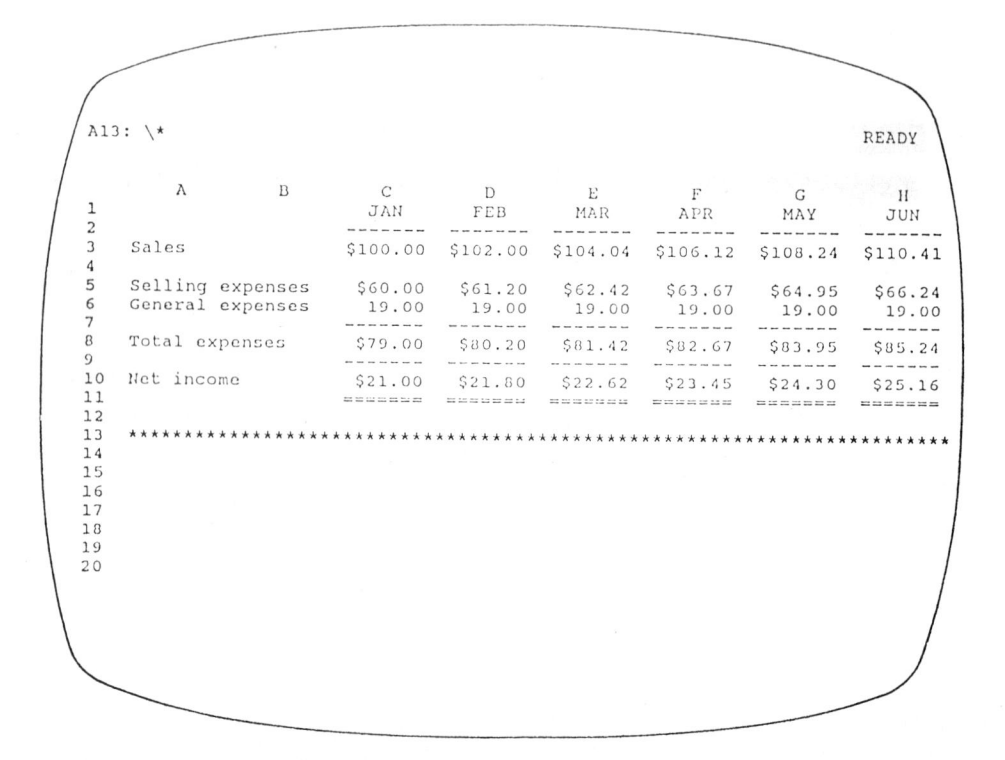

```
A13: \*                                                              READY

         A          B        C         D         E         F         G         H
 1                          JAN       FEB       MAR       APR       MAY       JUN
 2                         -------   -------   -------   -------   -------   -------
 3     Sales              $100.00   $102.00   $104.04   $106.12   $108.24   $110.41
 4
 5     Selling expenses    $60.00    $61.20    $62.42    $63.67    $64.95    $66.24
 6     General expenses     19.00     19.00     19.00     19.00     19.00     19.00
 7                         -------   -------   -------   -------   -------   -------
 8     Total expenses      $79.00    $80.20    $81.42    $82.67    $83.95    $85.24
 9                         -------   -------   -------   -------   -------   -------
10     Net income          $21.00    $21.80    $22.62    $23.45    $24.30    $25.16
11                         =======   =======   =======   =======   =======   =======
12
13     ************************************************************************
14
15
16
17
18
19
20
```

the screen simultaneously. Your worksheet should appear as shown in Illustration 7. Before going any further, save your new worksheet as SAMPLE2. (Type **/FS SAMPLE2**.)

Now try a column width of 15. Note that only four columns appear on the screen. Next, try a column width of 5. Here there is a surprise. You can probably guess what happened. The columns became too narrow to present the numbers and labels fully. Now try a column width of 9. As you can see from the result, the column width choice does not affect actual cell contents. It simply affects the screen presentation.

Global Recalculation (/WGR)

You can control the order in which 1-2-3 performs its calculations. The three options are Columnwise, Rowwise, or Natural. Columnwise means that the computer begins calculations in cell A1, moves down column A, then moves to cell B1, goes down that column, and so forth. Rowwise, as you might expect, begins calculations in cell A1 and then, moving left to right, moves down the worksheet row by row. 1-2-3 normally recalculates in the method called Natural. Under this method, 1-2-3 evaluates the worksheet to determine the most appropriate starting cell and sequence of cells for performing calculations. In your income statement the order of recalculation is not important, but in some worksheets it is.

The Recalculation options for Automatic, Manual, and Iteration relate to when recalculation occurs. Automatic is the way the program recalculates now. Any time a new number (input) is entered in cell C3, many of the other numbers are changed automatically. On larger worksheets with many inputs, you may wish to change several inputs before the recalculation occurs. You can change the recalculation from Automatic to Manual. In the Manual mode, you have to tell the computer when to recalculate the numbers.

To demonstrate this, type **/WGRM**. Next, enter the number **200** in cell C3 and press ENTER. What happens to the other numbers? Nothing, right? Now push the F9 key on the left side of the keyboard, and you will see the recalculation occur. You must press the F9 key each time you want a recalculation of your formulas when you are in the Manual mode.

The Iteration command will not be demonstrated here. The computer normally recalculates a worksheet only once after each input change. The Iteration option allows you to tell the computer to recalculate a worksheet several times with each change in input.

Type **/WGRA** now. That will get you back to the Automatic mode. Reset the value in cell C3 to **100**.

Global Protection (/WGP)

Your worksheet is currently unprotected, meaning that any cell's contents can be changed. You may, however, want to protect your worksheet or certain portions of it from accidental change. Since this 1-2-3 feature is mainly used to protect a specific

Illustration 7
Income Statement with a Column Width of 8 Characters (Saved as SAMPLE2)

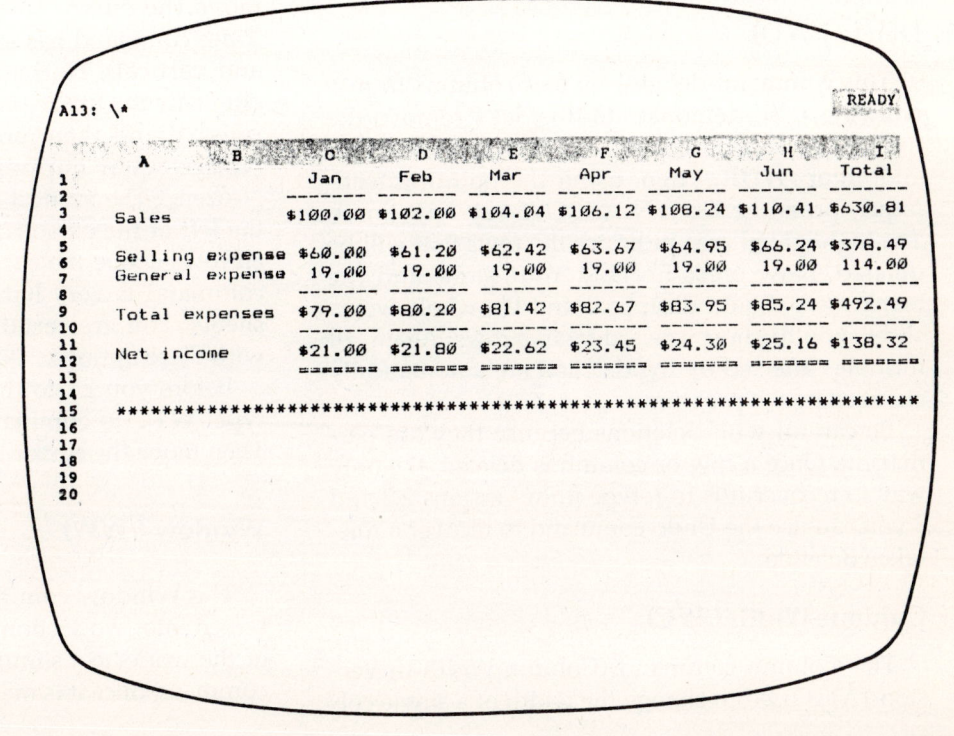

```
A13: \*                                                                 READY

        A         B        C        D        E        F        G        H         I
                          Jan      Feb      Mar      Apr      May      Jun      Total
 1
 2                        -------  -------  -------  -------  -------  -------  -------
 3     Sales             $100.00  $102.00  $104.04  $106.12  $108.24  $110.41  $630.81
 4
 5     Selling expense   $60.00   $61.20   $62.42   $63.67   $64.95   $66.24   $378.49
 6     General expense   19.00    19.00    19.00    19.00    19.00    19.00    114.00
 7                        -------  -------  -------  -------  -------  -------  -------
 8
 9     Total expenses    $79.00   $80.20   $81.42   $82.67   $83.95   $85.24   $492.49
10                        -------  -------  -------  -------  -------  -------  -------
11     Net income        $21.00   $21.80   $22.62   $23.45   $24.30   $25.16   $138.32
12                        =======  =======  =======  =======  =======  =======  =======
13
14
15     ******************************************************************************
16
17
18
19
20
```

range of cells, this command will be demonstrated later in conjunction with the **Range Protect** and **Range Unprotect** commands.

Global Zero (/WGZ)

Cells that have a value of zero are shown as blank cells if this command is used. This option is not available on Version 1A.

Insert (/WI)

This command is used to insert new columns or rows into a worksheet. Suppose you wish to insert your name at the top of the income statement. Right now there is no place at the top of the worksheet to do this. Let's add another row to the worksheet.

Position the cursor in row 1 (the column doesn't matter), enter **/WI**, press **R** to indicate "Row", and press ENTER to accept the computer's offer of the range. Instantly, the whole worksheet moves down a row so you can type your name! Now position the cursor in cell A1 and type your name.

If you want to insert several rows, you can override the computer's range offer by typing (or pointing to) your own range. For example, suppose you want to insert four more rows at the top of the worksheet. Press **/WIR** now and press the DOWN ARROW key three times. Finally, press ENTER. Instantly, four more rows are added to the statement.

The Insert command works for inserting rows and columns anywhere on the worksheet. It should also be noted that all formulas affected by an insertion are automatically changed by the program.

Delete (/WD)

This command deletes rows or columns from a worksheet. To demonstrate this, let's remove the five rows inserted above. Move the cursor to row 1 and enter **/WDR**. Then, using the pointing technique, press the DOWN ARROW key four times. The highlighted area indicates the rows that will be deleted. Now press ENTER. Your name and the blank rows should disappear and the whole worksheet should adjust upward by five rows. Again, all formulas affected by the deletion are automatically changed by the program.

Be careful with deletions because they are permanent. Once a row or column is deleted, the only way to recover it is to retype it. In Versions 2.2 and 3 you can use the Undo command to recover a mistaken deletion.

Column-Width (/WC)

The **Column** command (Column-Width in Version 1A) is used to change the width of a single column on the worksheet. This is more like a **Range** command than a **Worksheet** command. To demonstrate this command, move the cursor to cell C2 and type **/WC**. Press **S** to set the width of the current column (column C). Rather than accept the computer's offer, type the number **15** and press ENTER. Notice that column C is now 15 characters wide.

Next let's change the width of all the worksheet columns using the **Global** command. Type **/WGC5** and press ENTER. As you can see, although the other columns are now 5 characters wide, column C remains 15 characters wide. The **/WC** command sets the column width for a specific column and it cannot be altered by changes in global column width.

To return column C to the global width (5), type **/WC** and this time press **R** (for Reset). Before moving on, enter **/WGC9** to get back to the original format.

Titles (/WT)

The Titles command and the Window command (discussed below) are used to enhance the screen display of worksheets. The Titles command is used to "lock in" a row or column (or both) so that it always stays on the screen no matter where the cursor is. Move the cursor to cell A1. Notice that you cannot see the TOTAL column (column I) on the screen. You can pull column I onto the screen by moving the cursor to that column but then you lose column A.

To demonstrate the use of the Titles command, move the cursor to cell C1 and enter **/WT**. The Titles command has four options: **Both** (horizontal and vertical), **Horizontal**, **Vertical**, and **Clear** (to eliminate the freeze on all rows and columns). Now press **V** and then move the cursor to column L. Notice what happens. Columns A and B are "frozen." The vertical option freezes all columns to the left of the cursor. The horizontal option freezes all rows above the cursor. As you can imagine, this command is very handy for viewing large worksheets. You are certainly welcome to experiment with these options.

Before you go to the next command, be sure to type **/WTC** to eliminate any fixed titles you have. Then move the cursor to cell A1.

Window (/WW)

The Window command allows you to split the screen into two sections and view separate portions of the worksheet simultaneously. It is a very useful command once it is mastered.

166 Lotus 1-2-3 Tutorial

Let's use the Window command to view the edges of the income statement (e.g., column A and column I) simultaneously. Move the cursor to column D and enter /WW. You are now presented with five options: Horizontal, Vertical, Sync (both windows scroll together), Unsync, and Clear.

Press the letter V. What you see now is the screen split vertically. Press the F6 key several times and you will see the cursor jump from the left window to the right window and back again. Move the cursor to the right window. Then use the RIGHT ARROW key to move the cursor to column I. You can now see both edges of the income statement at once!

The primary advantage of the Window command is that it allows you to enter some input in a cell at one edge of the worksheet and see the immediate effect in a cell at the other edge. For example, suppose you want to know what your January sales level must be for total net income for the six-month period (cell I10) to be at least $150. Right now your six-month total is only $138.32, so you know that your January sales must be higher than $100. Although you can solve this particular problem mathematically, you can also solve it fairly quickly by trial and error using this program.

To solve this problem, press the F6 key to put the cursor in the left window. Then move the cursor to cell C3. Enter a new sales figure and press ENTER. Is the resulting total net income figure in cell I10 too high or too low? Enter a new figure in cell C3 to try again. After four or five quick tries you should be reasonably close to the answer. (The answer is that January sales must be at least $104.63 for total net income to be at least $150.)

To demonstrate the Sync subcommand (synchronized windows), move the cursor to the right window. Then move the cursor down to row 25. What happens to the alignment of the rows on the income statement? The right window and the left window scroll together. This is called synchronization. Now type /WWU. This will unsynchronize the two windows. Move the cursor up to row 1 again. The right window scrolls but the left window doesn't.

Type /WWC to eliminate the two windows, and then move the cursor to cell A1.

Status (/WS)

Type /WS now. The result is a status report on all of the Global settings. Although some of the settings are given in code, you can probably decipher them easily. Press the ESC key when you have finished examining this report.

RANGE COMMANDS

Range commands affect specific portions of the worksheet. The subcommands for Format (/RF) and Label-Prefix (/RL) have already been discussed. Most of the remaining Range commands will be discussed here. As mentioned in Lesson 2, when prompted by Range commands to specify cells in a range, there are four basic responses:

1. Accept the computer's offer and press ENTER.
2. Point to the range of your choice.
3. Type in the range of your choice.
4. Press ESC or CTRL BREAK to stop the command from being executed.

These responses were discussed and demonstrated in Lesson 2 and they will be used in this section.

Erase (/RE)

This command erases the contents of one cell or a range of cells. Although pressing the SPACE BAR and then ENTER will clear a cell, it does not truly erase the cell's entire contents. Although you cannot see the difference, the computer has stored a space bar for that cell in its memory. So, to erase the contents of a cell or range of cells completely, the Range Erase command should be used.

To demonstrate this command, let's erase some of the worksheet now. Suppose you wish to erase the word JAN. Move the cursor to cell C1 and enter /RE. The computer's suggestion is to erase C1 only. Let's accept the computer's offer. Press ENTER, and JAN disappears. To demonstrate erasing several cells, let's erase the rest of the month titles and the underlining. With the cursor still in cell C1, press /RE, move the cursor to cell H2, and press ENTER. The contents of these cells are immediately erased.

The Range Erase command is extremely helpful for correcting errors when designing spreadsheet models. Be careful with this command, however, because once something has been erased, it is gone! Rather than retype everything to get your completed model back on the screen, just reload it from the disk. To do this, type /FR SAMPLE and press ENTER. Your completed income statement should reappear on the screen.

Name (/RN)

This command allows you to give a range a specific name (e.g., SALES, JEAN, XY). The name may

Lotus 1-2-3 Tutorial 167

be up to 15 characters long. Later, any time you are asked to enter a range, you may specify the range by typing the name rather than typing the cell references.

To demonstrate the Range Name command, type **/RN** now. Next, type **C** to Create a name, then type the name **SALES**, and press ENTER. To indicate the cells that are included in the range, type **C3.I3** and press ENTER. Now, any time you wish to do something to this group of cells, you can indicate the range by typing the word **SALES** instead of the cell coordinates. As an example, suppose you wish to change the values in that range to integers (Currency format with zero decimal places). Type **/RFC0** and press ENTER. For the range, type **SALES** and press ENTER. The specified cells should now be expressed as integers.

To return the values to their original format, type **/RFC2** and press ENTER. To indicate the range, press the F3 key. In the control panel you now see the name SALES highlighted. If you had previously named other ranges, their names would appear as well. You would move the menu pointer to the proper name and press ENTER. In this case there is only one name, so just press ENTER and the range named SALES will be put back to its original format.

Range names are saved when the file is saved. To keep the range name SALES, you should save this file now. Type **/FS SAMPLE** and press ENTER. Then press **R** to indicate that you wish to Replace the old file with the new.

Justify (/RJ)

This command is a word processing feature of 1-2-3. Suppose you have typed a paragraph of instructions at the top of a spreadsheet model. Later, you revise the instructions by deleting and adding words, and you end up with a very ragged looking paragraph. You can then use the Range Justify command to reposition the words in the paragraph so that all lines begin at the left side of the range you specify.

Protect (/RP) and Unprotect (/RU)

The Range Protect and Range Unprotect commands are used to protect (or unprotect) specific portions of the worksheet. These commands work only after the Worksheet Global Protection Enable (**/WGPE**) command has been entered. In other words, the worksheet protection system must be turned on before these two Range subcommands can be used.

Let's work through an example to see how these commands are used. Enter **/WGPE** to turn on the worksheet protection feature. Move the cursor to cell C4, type the word **PIRATE**, and press ENTER. A noisy little beep and a message in the lower left corner of the screen tell you that this cell is protected; you cannot change its contents. In fact, at this point, all cells are protected. Press ESC or ENTER now to clear your entry.

If you want to answer what-if questions with your model, you will have to unprotect one or more cells so that you can enter proposed changes. On your income statement model, cell C3 is an important cell; if it were unprotected, you could perform what-if analysis. Move the cursor to cell C3, type **/RU**, and press ENTER to accept the program's range offer. Notice that the cursor in the unprotected cell is highlighted. You can now play what-if by changing the value in C3 without accidentally harming other parts of your model.

In some worksheets there may be several key input cells that you want unprotected. You can unprotect any range of cells in the same way you unprotected the single cell.

After unprotecting a cell, you may find circumstances where you wish to re-protect it. Let's do that with cell C3 now. Move the cursor to cell C3, enter the command **/RP**, and press ENTER. Cell C3 is now protected again and you cannot change its contents.

Before moving on to the next section, the entire model should be unprotected so that the subcommands in the remaining sections of this tutorial can be demonstrated. To turn off protection, type the command **/WGPD**. This disables the protection feature.

You can always check to see whether the protection is off or on by entering the Worksheet Status command. Enter that command now. You should find the word OFF or DISABLED next to Global Protection (or under the word Protect for Version 1A). Then press ESC or ENTER.

Input (/RI)

This command is an extension of the cell protection feature of 1-2-3. It restricts the cursor movement to a specified range of unprotected cells.

MOVE COMMAND (/M)

This command allows you to move a range of cells to another location on the worksheet. Two examples will be provided here. The first example demonstrates moving a range to a blank range. The second example involves moving a range of cells to a range where the cells already contain data.

First, suppose that you want to move the TOTAL column (column I) to the center of the screen below the monthly income statements. Move the cursor to cell I1 and press /**M**. Now press the DOWN ARROW key ten times to expand the FROM range from I1 to I11, then press ENTER. The program responds by asking for the range to move TO. Move the cursor to cell E14 and press ENTER again. In a flash, the move is completed! Note that you only had to indicate the beginning cell in the TO range.

Now let's move the TOTAL column back to its original location using the typing method. With the cursor still in cell I1, enter /**M**, type **E14.E24** as the range to move FROM, and press ENTER. Next, type the beginning cell location of the range to move TO (**I1**). Since the computer is already offering this as a suggestion, simply press ENTER. Instantly, the TOTAL column moves back.

To demonstrate the second kind of move, let's switch GENERAL EXPENSES and SELLING EXPENSES. This will take a little more maneuvering than the previous case because when you move a range to another location, the computer will overwrite the contents of any cells underneath. Move the cursor to cell A5 and insert a blank row (/**WIR** and press ENTER). This moves SELLING EXPENSES to row 6. Next, move the cursor to cell A7, enter /**M**, press the RIGHT ARROW key eight times to complete the FROM range, and press ENTER. Then move the cursor up to cell A5 and press ENTER to complete the TO range. Finally, with the cursor still in cell A7, enter /**WDR** and press ENTER to delete the extra row. The switch is now complete.

It is important to note that all formulas affected by a move are automatically changed by the program.

PRINT COMMANDS (/P)

You will now use the **Print** command to print the income statement from SAMPLE2, using the printer attached to your computer. If you do not have a printer hooked up to your computer, skip this section for now. You can always come back to it later.

The **Print** command requires that you have properly installed the hardware configuration on your disks. Please see your instructor if you have problems. Once the hardware configuration has been properly installed, you should find the **Print** command very simple to execute. The basic steps for printing the worksheet SAMPLE2 are as follows:

1. Turn the printer on and make sure it is "On Line."
2. Load the file to be printed (/**FR SAMPLE2**).
3. Press the SLASH key and then type **P** to select the **Print** option.
4. In response to **Printer** or **File**, press **P** to indicate **Printer**.
5. Press **R** to indicate your selection of Range.
6. Enter the range to be printed (either by pointing or typing) and press ENTER. In this case, either type **A1.I11** to indicate the corners and press ENTER; or press HOME, press the PERIOD (.) key, press END, press HOME again, and press ENTER.
7. If necessary, press **L** (Line) several times to position the paper in the printer so that the printing begins at the top of a page.
8. Press **A** (Align). This command tells the printer to align the top of the worksheet with the top of the page in the printer.
9. Press **G** to **G**o (begin printing). The printer should now spring to life and print out the worksheet exactly as you see it on the screen.
10. Press **P** (Page) to eject the page just printed from the printer.
11. When you are done with the **Print** command, press **Q** to **Q**uit.

If you cannot get your printer to work, refer to the Lotus 1-2-3 manual or contact your instructor for more detailed assistance. Also, see Appendix C (Resolving Problems) of this manual for some additional suggestions.

Should you wish to halt the printing before it finishes the range you have specified, press the CTRL and BREAK keys simultaneously to stop the printing. The Mode Indicator will change from WAIT to READY, but some printers will print a few more lines before stopping.

Many printers will print up to 80 characters per line, about the same as a typewriter. Lotus 1-2-3 is designed to print 72 characters per line, which is the width of the worksheet seen on the monitor. Each line on your income statement in the file SAMPLE2 contains 72 characters, 9 columns (A through I) times 8 characters per column. If you are printing a worksheet that is wider than 72 characters (such as SAMPLE), the additional columns will be printed automatically on later pages. Although not discussed in this tutorial, there are many print options available to alter borders, margins, page length, etc. This is done by selecting "Options" from the print menu.

The PRTSC key on the IBM PC can be used in a limited fashion to print spreadsheet models. When the PRTSC key and the SHIFT key are pressed simultaneously, the printer will print all data shown on the screen. Try it now. You will note that it prints the worksheet borders, too.

GRAPH COMMANDS (/G)

These commands allow you to display spreadsheet figures graphically on your screen. This is a very exciting part of Lotus 1-2-3, but not all IBM PC's have the capability of displaying graphics. You need both a graphics display screen and a graphics card to use this command. If you are unsure how your machine is configured, you may try the steps outlined in this section anyway. When you get to the final step, if the Mode Indicator flashes WAIT for several seconds, your IBM PC is not equipped to handle graphics. You should then press ESC to kill the command and go on to the next section.

The Graph commands are extensive, so all that will be attempted here is to expose you to some basic commands. Type /G. From the menu of subcommands, select **X**. You will be asked to enter the X-axis range. Move the cursor to cell C1 (JAN), press the period (.) key, press the RIGHT ARROW key five times to expand the range to cell H1 (JUN), and press ENTER. Next, from the menu of subcommands, select **A**. You will be asked to enter the first data range. Move the cursor to cell C3, press the PERIOD (.) key, press the RIGHT ARROW key five times to expand the range to cell H3, and press ENTER. Finally, from the menu of subcommands, select **B**. You will be asked to enter the second data range. Move the cursor to cell C8, press the PERIOD (.) key, press the RIGHT ARROW key five times to expand the range to cell H8, and press ENTER.

From the menu of subcommands, select **View**. What you should see now is a line graph plotting monthly sales and expenses. This is one of several graph options. When you are done examining the line graph, press ESC or ENTER. Now select **Type** from the subcommand list, and enter **B** for **Bar** Graph. Press **V** once more and a bar chart appears on the screen. Go ahead and experiment with the other graph options. When done, press **Q** to **Quit**.

Once the basic graphics options have been selected, you can press the **F10** key any time you are in the READY mode, and the graph will immediately be displayed on the screen. This feature allows you to perform what-if graphing. Each time you enter new values in a data range, pressing **F10** will let you graphically see the impact immediately.

QUIT (/Q)

This command will end your 1-2-3 session and get you back to the Lotus Access System Menu. Unless you need to get to this menu, see page 155 for detailed instructions.

FORMULA POINTING

The 1-2-3 program provides an alternate way to enter formulas. The pointing technique can be used any time you use a cell reference in a formula. It can be used with all arithmetic operations. Instead of typing the cell references, pointing allows you to use the ARROW keys to point to the cells you want to enter. Some people make extensive use of pointing; others use it only occasionally.

To demonstrate pointing, follow the steps below:

1. Load SAMPLE2, if it is not already on the screen.
2. Move the cursor to cell G14.
3. Type the PLUS SIGN (+).
4. Move the cursor to cell C3.
5. Type the MINUS SIGN (-).
6. Move the cursor to cell C8.
7. Press ENTER.

The net income for January should now appear in cell G14.

FORMATTING NEW FILE DISKS

Instead of storing models that you design on the Template Disk, you may wish to store them on a separate disk. The preparation of this additional storage disk should be done ahead of time because the initialization process wipes out whatever is on the screen.

To prepare your blank disk to store 1-2-3 files, use the following steps:

1. Obtain the IBM PC DOS or MS DOS disk.
2. Remove the Lotus System Disk from drive A and insert the DOS disk.
3. Depress the CRTL key and the ALT key. While holding these keys down press the DEL key. Doing this clears the program that is in memory (Lotus 1-2-3) and loads the operating system (DOS).

4. At the A>, type **FORMAT B:** and press ENTER.
5. Insert the blank disk in drive B and press ENTER.
6. When the formatting is done, press **N** in response to "Format Another?"
7. Remove the formatted disk from drive B and label it as "1-2-3 File Disk."

This completes Lesson 3! You may go on to Lesson 4 immediately if you wish. If you want to stop here, simply turn off the computer and remove both disks.

LESSON 4
SPECIAL FUNCTION COMMANDS

Special function commands are used to perform special calculations in cells. Each function is activated by pressing the AT (@) key.

This section is meant to be read but not necessarily worked through on the computer at this time. Use it as a reference guide as you solve the workbook problems.

@SUM(X.Y)

This function has already been described in Lesson 2. It is used to add numbers in a range beginning with cell X (any cell you wish) and ending with cell Y. For examples of how this function is used, refer to Lesson 2.

@SQRT(X)

This function will compute the square root of X. X can be a value or a cell reference. As a simple example, suppose you wish to compute the square root of 144 and enter the result in cell A5. Positioning the cursor in cell A5 and entering the following formula will accomplish this (remember that the cursor position is on the left followed by a colon):

A5:@SQRT(144)

Another example is as follows:

B8:@SQRT(A24)

In this case, you are telling 1-2-3 to take the square root of the value found in cell A24 and enter it in cell B8.

@MAX(list)

This function will return the maximum value found in a list of cells separated by commas, or in a specified range.

@MIN(list)

This function will return the minimum value found in a list of cells separated by commas, or in a specified range.

@ROUND(A,B)

This function will round the value A to the number of decimals specified by B. For example, if cell A80 contained the formula @ROUND(B71,2), the computer will round the value found in cell B71 to two decimal places and enter it in cell A80. This is different than using the **Range Format** command to format a cell to display numbers with two decimal places because the @ROUND command eliminates all values to the right of the decimal places specified. @ROUND(B71,0) will round the value found in cell B71 to zero decimal places (an integer).

Using this special function command would have eliminated the problem encountered in Lesson 2 (Numerical Input Errors) where a column of numbers did not add up correctly because of rounding errors.

@IF (CONDITION,A,B)

This function allows the program to choose one of two values to enter in a cell. If a specified condition is true, Value A will be put in the cell. If the condition is false, Value B will be entered. An example of how this function can be used is as follows:

C2:@IF(A8=2,7,9)

This formula states that if the value in cell A8 is equal to 2, enter a 7 in cell C2; if the value in cell A8 is not equal to 2, enter a 9 in cell C2.

The "conditions" that may be used are as follows:

=	equal to
>	greater than
<=	less than
<=	less than or equal to
>	greater than or equal to
<>	not equal to

Here are some other acceptable examples:

B12:	@IF(Bll>>B10,B11,B10)
D23:	@IF(A3<<A5,D8,D10/D11)
H71:	@IF(G12>>=0,0,@SUM(C20.C58))
F22:	@IF(A1=0,B7,@IF(A1=1,B8,B9))

@VLOOKUP(A,X.Y,C) and @HLOOKUP(A,X.Y,C)

These functions allow you to look up a value in a table. They are similar in concept to the @IF function, but they allow the program to pick an answer from a whole table of values.

For an example of how the **@VLOOKUP** function works, suppose you are setting up a 1-2-3 model to use in tax planning for your clients. As a

172   Lotus 1-2-3 Tutorial

part of the tax planning program, you want a client's tax bracket to be automatically computed based on his/her taxable income. You obtain the information in the following table from the Internal Revenue Service (hypothetical):

Taxable Income

Over	But Not Over	Tax Bracket
$ -0-	$ 5,000	15%
5,000	12,000	19
12,000	21,000	23
21,000	34,000	28
34,000	60,000	36
60,000	---	50

You can incorporate this table into your tax planning model by constructing the following table:

E40: INCOME	F40: BRACKET
E41: 0.00	F41: 15
E42: 5000.01	F42: 19
E43: 12000.01	F43: 23
E44: 21000.01	F44: 28
E45: 34000.01	F45: 36
E46: 60000.01	F46: 50

Now assume that the client's taxable income will be computed by your tax model and will be entered in cell G10. You wish to have the client's tax bracket automatically determined by the program and shown in cell G11. The following formula would be used:

G11:@VLOOKUP(G10,E41.F46,1)

The **@VLOOKUP** function takes the value from cell G10 and searches for a corresponding value in the income column of the table. This is called the comparison column. The search begins in cell E41 and ends when a value greater than the value in cell G10 is found. The program then returns to the next lower value in column E, picks up the number found in the corresponding cell one column to its immediate right (the data column), and enters it in cell G11.

The range of cells entered in the middle of the **@VLOOKUP** formula begins with the top of the comparison column and ends with the bottom of the last data column. Lookup tables can have more than one data column. The "1" in the formula for G11 indicates that the answer is found in the first data column to the right of the comparison column.

As an example, suppose the taxable income value found in cell G10 is 10000. In evaluating cell G11, the program would jump to cell E41 and begin looking for a value greater than 10000. The first cell containing a value greater than 10000 is cell E43 (it contains 12000). The program then returns to cell E42 (the next lower value cell), picks up the corresponding value in one column to the right (19), and enters it in cell G11.

Note the following three things about the **@VLOOKUP** and **@HLOOKUP** functions:

1. If the value being searched for is less than the lowest number in the table, the program will indicate this by returning "ERR." In our example, this is what would happen if the value of G10 were less than zero.
2. The table must always be constructed in ascending order.
3. The table may be constructed in rows instead of columns. If rows are used, the **@HLOOKUP** function is utilized. The top row is searched (left to right) and the bottom row contains the value that is returned.

@NPV(I,X.Y)

This function will automatically compute the net present value of annual future cash flows (represented by cells X through Y) discounted at the interest rate I. The interest rate I may be expressed as a number or as a cell reference.

Suppose that an investment's projected future cash inflows for each of the next three years are entered in cells D38, E38, and F38. Also suppose that you wish to compute the present value of these future cash flows using a discount rate of 11%. You want the result to be put in cell H14. The following formula will accomplish this:

H14:@NPV(.11,D38.F38)

If the discount rate is found in cell B2, one of the following formulas will work:

H14:@NPV(B2,D38.F38)

or **H14:@NPV(B2/100,D38.F38)** if B2 is an integer

If a cash outlay is necessary at the beginning of the first year to acquire this investment, the cash outlay (found in cell G12) can be subtracted from the formula as follows:

H14:@NPV(B2,D38.F38)-G12

As with the **@SUM** function, when a period (.) is entered between D38 and F38, the computer will respond with two periods.

@IRR(guess,X.Y)

This function will approximate the internal rate of return for a series of cash flows (represented by cells X through Y). To start the process, you must enter an initial guess (from 0.00 to 1.0) either as a number or as a cell reference.

Suppose that an investment's projected cash flows, entered in cells B17 through B21, are -$200,000; $60,000; $60,000; $75,000; and $75,000. Also suppose that you want the IRR to be entered in cell C6. Your initial guess will be 13%. The formula is as follows:

C6:@IRR(.13,B17.B21)

If your initial guess is found in cell B3, one of the following formulas will work:

C6:@IRR(B3,B17.B21)
or C6:@IRR(B3/100,B17.B21) if B3 is an integer

@PMT(P,I,T)

This function will compute the periodic payment amount needed to pay back a loan of P dollars at an interest rate I over a period of time T. T is the number of payments to be made and I is always expressed as the interest rate per payment. For example, @PMT(100000,.11,10) would compute the annual payment needed to retire a $100,000 loan at 11% interest over ten years (the answer is $16,980.14). If the payments were to be made monthly, the formula should be written as @PMT(100000,.11/12,120) (the answer is $1,377.50). As with all other special function commands, cell references may be used in place of values anywhere in the formula.

@FV(A,I,T)

This function computes the future value of an ordinary annuity. A is the amount of the periodic payment and is assumed to occur at the end of the period. I is the interest rate per payment, and T represents the number of payments made. For example, if at the end of each year you put $100 into a savings account earning 5% interest, how much would the account yield at the end of the fifth year? The formula @FV(100,.05,5) provides the answer ($552.56).

@PV(A,I,T)

This function computes the present value of an ordinary annuity where A is the annuity amount, I is the interest rate per payment, and T is the number of payments made. For example, @PV(100,.08,7) would compute the present value of $100 payments to be made at the end of each of the next seven years discounted at an annual rate of 8% (the answer is $520.63).

Functions Used in Calculations

Each of the preceding functions is used to compute a value to be entered in a cell. Functions may be linked with other standard arithmetic operations and can also be combined with one another. All of the following are legitimate 1-2-3 formulas:

D16: +D15/@VLOOKUP(C12,E4.F9,1)
A41: @SUM(B12.H12)+17
A42: +A17*@IF(B1=0,2,B9)
D18: @IF(H16>>12,0,@MAX(H2.H9))

Pointing

As a reminder, anytime a cell reference is used in one of these special functions, it can be entered by typing it in or by using the ARROW keys to "point" to the cell and then pressing ENTER.

Other Functions

The 1-2-3 program contains many more functions than those covered here. The ones chosen for discussion in this lesson are the most commonly used functions. You are certainly encouraged to review a more advanced 1-2-3 tutorial to learn about other functions. A partial listing of these functions is found in Appendix B of this workbook.

This completes the 1-2-3 tutorial. You are encouraged at this point to read Appendix C of this workbook. It provides a good review of common errors made by beginners.

APPENDIX A
START-UP PROCEDURES

Operating a microcomputer is fairly easy. With a few simple instructions, you should have no problems at all.

IBM PC HARDWARE

An IBM PC system consists of a keyboard, a processing unit containing one or two floppy disk drives, and a monitor (TV screen). If there are two drives, the drive on the left (or on top) is drive A, and the one on the right (or on the bottom) is drive B. If there is a hard disk drive, it is referred to as drive C. A printer may be attached to the system.

LOADING A PROGRAM

Computer programs are usually stored on disks. Loading a program means transferring the program from the disk to the processing unit. To load a program, use the following steps:

1. Before a program can be loaded, the disk operating system (DOS) must be loaded into the computer. This requires a separate DOS disk or a program disk that has had DOS placed on it. For example, DOS can be placed on Version 1A of Lotus 1-2-3 but not on Versions 2, 2.2, or 3. Insert the disk with DOS on it (either a separate DOS disk or a program disk) into drive A. If the latch over the slot in the drive is closed, open it. The disk should be inserted with the label upwards. The edge of the disk with the oval cutout in the disk's square plastic cover should enter the drive first. The edge with the label should enter the drive last. A good rule to follow is to hold the disk with your thumb on the label.
Push the disk gently until it is entirely into the drive. If you bend or force the disk, it can be permanently damaged. Close the disk drive latch. Never turn on the computer without a disk in the drive.
2. Turn on the computer. The switch is located on the right side of the processing unit toward the back. Also, make sure the monitor is on.

The red light on the disk drive will come on and the drive will make a lot of clacking and spinning noises. After a while, the red light will go out and you may need to enter some information from the keyboard (for example, date and time). After each entry, press the large key with the (⏎) symbol. This key is referred to as the ENTER key throughout this manual. The red light may go on and off several more times. If you used a program disk with DOS already on it, the program will now be loaded in the computer and will be ready to run. If you used a separate DOS disk, you will see the operating system prompt (A>) on the screen. This manual uses A> to represent the operating system prompt, but your prompt may look different. Remove the DOS disk and insert the program disk. Type the name of the program and press ENTER. The program will then be loaded.

CARE OF DISKS

Magnetic data is stored on the disk and is read by heads within the disk drive positioned over the oval cutout on the disk's cover. Never touch the magnetic tape surfaces of the disk. Never let it get greasy, dirty, or dusty. Always handle the disk by the black plastic cover only. When a disk is not in use, keep it in the paper pocket in which it came. Do not write on the disk label except with a felt-tip pen. Keep the disks away from magnetic fields such as TV screens and electric motors. Disks are also sensitive to extremes of temperature.

AN ASSURING NOTE

With most commercial software (programs), you do not have to worry about mistakenly touching the wrong keys on the computer. You may end up entering weird data into the computer, but this usually can be corrected by entering the proper data later. Nothing you enter will wreck the programs or the computer. If things get too mixed up, you can just turn off the computer and start over!

APPENDIX B

LOTUS 1-2-3 COMMAND SUMMARY

/COMMANDS	EXPLANATION
/WGF	Global formats for values (fixed, general, percent, etc.)
/WGL	Global label alignment (left, right, center)
/WGC	Global change of all column widths
/WGR	Global recalculation (natural, rowwise, manual, etc.)
/WGP	Turn global protection on or off
/WGD	Global default configurations
/WGZ	Global suppression of zeros (Versions 2 and 2.01 only)
/WIC	Insert blank column(s)
/WIR	Insert blank row(s)
/WDC	Delete column(s)
/WDR	Delete row(s)
/WC	Set column width of current column
/WE	Erase worksheet from the screen
/WTB	Horizontal and vertical title freeze
/WTH	Horizontal title freeze
/WTV	Vertical title freeze
/WTC	Eliminate frozen titles
/WWH	Split screen horizontally (window)
/WWV	Split screen vertically (window)
/WWS	Synchronized scrolling of windows
/WWU	Unsynchronized scrolling of windows
/WWC	Eliminate split screen
/WS	Display worksheet settings
/WP	Places a page marker on the worksheet for the printer to use (all versions but 1A)
/RF	Format a cell or range of cells (fixed, general, etc.)
/RL	Label alignment for a cell or range of cells (left, right, center)
/RE	Erase a cell or range of cells
/RN	Name a cell or range of cells
/RJ	Place a written paragraph into a given range
/RP	Protect a cell or range of cells from accidental erasure or entry
/RU	Eliminate protection on a cell or range of cells
/C	Copy a cell or range of cells
/M	Move a cell or range of cells
/FR	Retrieve (load) a file from disk
/FS	Save a file on disk
/FEW	Erase worksheet file from disk
/FL	List of files on disk
/PPR	Set range to be printed
/PPL	Line feed
/PPP	Page feed
/PPO	Printout options (header, margins, border, etc.)
/PPC	Reset printer options
/PPA	Tell 1-2-3 to begin new page at current type head position
/PPG	Print the worksheet
/PPQ	End print session; return to READY mode
/PF	Prints to a text file on disk
/GT	Set graph type (line, bar, pie, etc.)
/GX	Set X-axis labels
/GA	Establish first data set to be displayed

/COMMANDS	EXPLANATION
/GB	Establish second data set to be displayed
/GV	View the graph on the screen
/DF	Fills a given range with sequential values
/DT	Develops a table of selected what-if results
/DS	Sorts data in ascending or descending order
/DQ	Locates data in database meeting specified criteria
/S	Exit to DOS (Versions 2 and 2.01 only)
/A	Allows access to programs written by developers (Version 2.2 only)
/Q	Quit 1-2-3 session

KEYBOARD COMMANDS	EXPLANATION
F1	Help screens
F2	Edit contents of cell
F3	Select a range name from a list of all range names
F4	Establish "absolute" cell address when pointing
F5	Move cursor to specified location on worksheet
F6	Move cursor between windows
F7	Repeat most recent data query operation
F8	Select last chosen table range for data table command
F9	Force recalculation
F10	In the READY mode, redraw most recent graph
ALT-F4	Undo feature reverses or cancels last command sequence entered (Versions 2.2 and 3)
ESC	Cancel current entry
CTRL BREAK	Cancel current operation
(↵)	Backspace
PG UP	Move screen up 20 lines
PG DN	Move screen down 20 lines
(→)	Tab right; move screen right one page
(←)	Tab left; move screen left one page (with SHIFT key)
HOME	Move cursor to cell A1
END	Use with ARROW keys to move cursor to end of active area
END HOME	Move cursor to lower right corner of worksheet
NUM LOCK	Use numbers from the keypad
PRTSC	Print out of computer screen
"	Right aligned label
'	Left aligned label
^	Centered label
\	Repeating label

FUNCTION COMMANDS	EXPLANATION
@ABS(x)	Absolute value of x
@AVG(list)	Average value of list
@CHOOSE(x,a.b)	Choose Xth value from list
@COS(x)	Cosine of x expressed in radians
@COUNT(list)	Count nonblank cells in list
@DATE(yy,mm,dd)	Date
@FV(x,i,t)	Future value of an ordinary annuity
@HLOOKUP(x,a.b,y)	Look up values in a horizontal table
@IF(cond,x,y)	If condition is true, enter x; otherwise enter y
@INT(x)	Integer value of x

FUNCTION COMMANDS	EXPLANATION
@IRR(x,a.b)	Internal rate of return
@LN(x)	Natural log of x
@MAX(list)	Maximum value in list
@MIN(list)	Minimum value in list
@NPV(x,a.b)	Net present value
@PMT(p,i,t)	Payment needed to amortize investment or debt
@PV(x,i,t)	Present value of an ordinary annuity
@RAND	Random number between 0 and 1
@ROUND(x,n)	Round the value x to n decimal places
@SQRT(x)	Square root of value x
@STD(list)	Standard deviation of list values
@SUM(list)	Sum of list of values
@VLOOKUP(x,a.b,y)	Look up value x in a vertical table

Note: This is not a complete list of commands, keyboard commands, or @ functions.

APPENDIX C
RESOLVING PROBLEMS (What to Do When Things Go Wrong)

1. I can't get a spreadsheet file to load.

    — Check to make sure that the Lotus System Disk is in drive A and the Template Disk is in drive B. Files from your Template Disk will not load unless 1-2-3 is loaded first.
    — Check the tutorial to make sure that you are following the proper command sequence for loading files.
    — Make sure you are typing the EXACT name of the file.
    — Check the files list (**/FLW** and press ENTER) on the disk to make sure that the file you are trying to load is there.

2. I saved a file on the disk but now it is not there.

    — You may have misspelled the file name when saving it. Check the files list on the Template Disk to make sure that the file you are trying to load is there.
    — If the file name is not in the directory, the file was not properly saved. Unfortunately, you will have to start over. An infuriating mistake when saving a file is to type **/FR** instead of **/FS**. This reloads the old file instead of saving the new one. Ouch!

3. I cannot save my file.

    — If the mode indicator shows ERROR, see Number 8 below.
    — Make sure the Template Disk is properly inserted in drive B.
    — If the computer responds with "Disk is write protected," the disk you are trying to save your file to cannot be used for saving files. A common mistake is to place a write-protect tab over the notch on the Template Disk. This should not be done because it prevents saving new files on the disk.
    — If the computer responds with "Disk full," the disk is, in fact, full. One way to solve this dilemma is to delete one or more files on the disk to make room for the new file. Erasing files will not affect the worksheet currently in the computer's memory. Type **/FEW** and select the file to be deleted. When the deletion is completed, type **/FS** to save the new file.
    The other alternative is to use a new storage disk. If you have another disk properly formatted, simply insert that disk into drive B and save your file on it. If you do not have a disk that is formatted, you are out of luck if you are using Version 1A. You must exit the program to prepare a new disk for storage (see Lesson 3). If you have any other version of Lotus 1-2-3, type **/S** in the READY mode and follow the directions for formatting a disk in Lesson 3. This process will not exit you from the program.

4. I can't get the printer to work correctly.

    — Press CTRL and BREAK keys to kill the Print command or the flashing WAIT sign.
    — You may have forgotten to enter the print range. The computer will print nothing unless the print range is specified.
    — It may be a hardware problem. Make sure the printer is connected to the computer. Make sure the printer is turned on and that the Select button is on. The printer is not "on line" if either the Line Feed (LF) or the Form Feed (FF) buttons are activated.
    — It may be a system problem. Your computer may not be sending proper messages to your printer. With some printers, special codes must be sent to the printer before it will print spreadsheet files. Consult your instructor or the 1-2-3 manual for more specific instructions.
    — If the printing is in the wrong mode (i.e., compressed, proportional spacing, etc.), turn the printer off and then turn it back on again.

5. I can't load ANY files from the Template Disk.

    — Remove the Template Disk and then reinsert it in the drive. Sometimes a disk can get out of position and needs to be reseated.
    — The disk may have been damaged, soiled, or exposed to magnetic fields or extreme temperatures. See your instructor for replacement.

6. I mistakenly typed something in the wrong cell on a preprogrammed template.

    — If you haven't pressed ENTER, use the ESC key to eliminate the incorrect entry. The original cell contents will be restored automatically.
    — If you have already pressed ENTER
    - and the cell should be blank, type **/RE** and press ENTER to clear the cell.
    - and you have wiped out a preprogrammed label or number, simply retype the original contents in the cell. Refer to the printout of the template if necessary.

Lotus 1-2-3 Tutorial

— and you have wiped out a preprogrammed formula, retype it if possible. If this is not possible, you will have to start over by reloading (**/FR**) the file from the Template Disk.

7. The word ERR appears on my worksheet.

    — The word ERR will appear in any cell that has a formula containing a cell address for a cell that has been deleted. Suppose that the formula in cell A18 is +F9. Suppose also that you rearrange your model and delete row 9. This will cause an ERR message in cell A18. It will also cause an ERR message in any cell with a formula that contains the cell address A18. This situation can be corrected by redoing the formula in cell A18.

    — The word ERR will appear in any cell having a formula that requires dividing one value into another but where the denominator currently has a value of zero.

    — (Version 2 only) The word ERR will appear in any cell that has a formula referencing another cell that contains a label. This is not really an error. Entering a value in the referenced cell will remove the ERR indicator. If the ERR message is annoying to you, see the Lotus manual for instructions on correcting this.

8. The word ERROR appears in the mode indicator box.

    — Lotus 1-2-3 is designed to catch certain errors automatically. Check the lower left corner of the screen for a short message on the nature of the error. If you do not understand the message, you should look at the Lotus Reference Manual, which contains four pages of error message explanations. Press ESC or ENTER to continue working.

9. The word CIRC appears at the bottom of the screen.

    — The word CIRC will appear if your model has a "circular reference." For example, if cell D3 has the formula +E3 and cell E3 has the formula +D3, this is a circular reference. Circular references may involve only one cell (e.g., the formula in cell E7 is +E7), two cells, or more than two cells, and may be difficult to track down. The only way to correct a circular reference is to change the formulas in your model.

10. My worksheet loads with the cursor in a funny position.

    — When you save a spreadsheet model, the computer also saves the position of the cursor at the time the command is entered. To save the cursor in cell A1, position the cursor there by pressing the HOME key before saving the model.

11. A column of numbers does not add up.

    — This is not an error. 1-2-3 rounds numbers when displaying them on the screen. Sometimes this rounding process results in an addition being off by a small amount. To correct this, use the **@ROUND** command discussed in Lesson 4.

12. When I enter a decimal in a cell, the computer responds with a 0 (or a 1).

    — This is not an error. Many preprogrammed templates are designed with an integer format (**/WGFF0**). This means that decimals will be rounded. If you wish a decimal to show in a cell, format that cell to display decimals (for example, **/RFF2**) or use the **General** format (**/RFG**).

INDEX FOR
LOTUS 1-2-3 TUTORIAL

Absolute cell reference, 159
Addition, 152
Arithmetic calculations, 152-153
Arrow keys, 150,170

BACKSPLASH key, 157,162
BACKSPACE key, 152
Basic spreadsheet modeling, 156
Blank out a cell, 152
Borders, 162
BREAK, CONTROL, key, 154

Caret, 152
Cell,
   blank out a, 152
   copying, 158-159
   editing, contents, 152
   reference, absolute, 159
   reference, relative, 159
Clearing the screen, 154
Column width, 154,164,166
Combine, 163
Commands, 1-2-3, 153,176
   Copy, 153,158
   Data, 153
   File, 153,163
   Graph, 153
   Move, 153
   Print, 153
   Quit, 153
   Range, 153,157,167
   sequence of, 153
   special funtion, 172
   System, 153
   Worksheet, 153,154,157
Conditional function, 172
Control break, 154
Control Panel, 150
Copy command, 153,158-160
Copying cells, 158-159
   several cells at once, 159-160
Cursor movement, 150
   function key, 151
   other methods, 151

Data command, 153
Data entry, 151
Delete, 166
   a comamnd, 154
DEL key, 152
Directory, 163
Disk,
   formatting file, 170
   system, 149
   template, 10
Division, 153

Editing cell contents, 151-152
Electronic spreadsheet, 149
END key, 151
ENTER, 1
Erase, 163,167
Erase worksheet shortcut, 155
Error correction, 152
Escape (ESC), 150,152,154
Exponentiation, 153

File commands, 163
   Combine, 163
   Directory, 163
   Erase, 163,167
   Import, 163
   List, 163
   Retrieve, 163
   Save, 163
   Xtract, 163
File disks, formating, 170
File name Cancel Replace, 163
Format, Comma, 161
   Currency, 161
   Fixed, 161
   General, 161
   Hidden, 161
   Percent, 161
   Text, 161
Formatting, value range, 161
Formula method, 156
Formula pointing, 170
Formulas, 156
Function commands, 177
Functions, in calculations, 177
Future value of an ordinary annuity
   function, 177

Global Column-Width, 164
Global protectio, 165
Global recalculation, 165
Global zero, 166
Graph commands, 170

HELP key, 154
HOME key, 151

Import, 163
Input, 151,168
Insert, 166
Internal rate of return function, 177

Justify, 168

Keyboard commands, 177

Label, 151,152
Label alignment, 156

Label alignment, 156
   global, 157
   range, 157
   single cell, 157
LEFT ARROW key, 150
List, 163
Loading Lotus 1-2-3, 162
Lookup functions,
   horizontal, 177
   vertical, 178
Lotus Access System, 149

Maximum value function, 178
Menu, Lotus, 149
Menu pointer, 154
Minimum value function, 178
Mode Indicator, 149
Move command, 168
Multiplication, 153

Name, 167-168
Nested parentheses, 153
Net present value function, 178
Numerical input errors, 162
NUM LOC key, 151

Parentheses, nested, 153
PG DN key, 151
PG UP key, 151
Pointing, 158,170
   when copying cells, 159
Present value of an ordinary annuity
   function, 178
Print command, 169
Protect, 168
Problem solving, 179-180

Quit, 153,170

Range, 154
   commands, 157-158,167
   source, 158
   target, 158
READY mode 150,154
Recalculation, 165
   Automatic, 165
   Columnwise, 165
   Iteration, 165
   Manual, 165
   Natural, 165
   Rowwise, 165
Relative cell reference, 159
Retrieve, 163
RIGHT ARROW key, 150
Rounding function, 178

Save, 163

Screen, clearing, 154
Scrolling, 150
SHIFT key, 151
SLASH key, 153
Special function commands, 172
Spreadsheet, 149
    basic modeling, 156
Square root function, 178
Status, 167
Subcommands,
    Column-Width, 166
    Delete, 166
    Erase, 167
    Global, 164,165
    Insert, 166
    Status, 167
    Titles, 166

Window, 166
Subtraction, 153
Summation function, 156
Sync, 167
System command, 8
System disk, 149
System prompt, 149

TAB key, 151
Template disk, 163,179
Titles, 166

Underlines, 161
Unprotect, 168

Values, 151,152
View, 170

What-if analysis, 162
Window, 166
    Sync, 167
Workbook problem instructions, 179
Worksheet, 154
    commands, 164
    Erase command, 167
    setup, 156
    shortcut to erase, 155

Xtract, 163

Zero, 166